GUIDE TO

MICROCOMPUTERS

FRANZ J. FREDERICK

Association for Educational Communications and Technology
Washington, DC   1980

AECT-ERIC/Information Resources, Syracuse University

LC 80-68716
ISBN 0-89240-038-2

This work is the original work of the author. Authors are encouraged to express freely their judgments in professional and technical matters. Points of view or opinions do not necessarily represent the official view or opinion of AECT.

Additional copies of this book may be purchased by writing to:
AECT Publications Sales
1126 Sixteenth Street NW
Washington, DC 20036

This publication was prepared with funding from the National Institute of Education, U.S. Department of Education, under Contract No. NIE-400-77-0015. The opinions expressed in this report do not necessarily reflect the positions or policies of NIE or HEW.

Foreword

In 1964 AECT (then the Department of Audiovisual Instruction of the National Education Association) published its first monograph: *The Automation of School Information Systems*. The monograph, a book of readings edited by Don Bushnell, was accomplished in cooperation with the newly formed Association for Educational Data Systems. It was an early recognition of automation and computers as they were being used and were expected to be used in education and instruction. Since then, concern with computers evidenced by the membership of AECT has continued and grown. In 1972 a selected bibliography was published, *Computer Assisted Instruction: A Selected Bibliography* compiled by Dennis Barnes and Debra Schrieber.

The use of computers throughout our society has grown by leaps and bounds in the last twenty years. AECT is pleased to present this latest monograph, by Franz J. Frederick, in cooperation with the Educational Resources Information Clearinghouse on Instructional Resources at Syracuse University. Director Don Ely, an AECT Past President and current member of AECT's Nonperiodic Publications Board, has been most helpful in the development of this publication. We all owe him a debt of gratitude, and a greater debt to author Franz J. Frederick.

Most of us see a large role for the microcomputer in instruction in the years ahead. To help make that prophecy come true, this publication has been assembled for the educational community.

> Howard B. Hitchens
> *Executive Director*
> *Association for Educational Communications*
> *and Technology*

Contents

Presents a selected list of companies specializing in creating specialized languages and applications programs for microcomputers.

Presents a selected list of companies specializing in the preparation of educational programs for use on microcomputers.

CHAPTER 1

An Inside Look at Microcomputers

Education is privileged to be a witness to a revolution more far-reaching than that of the "printing press," and not just a witness, but potentially an integral part of the revolution. This revolution is the result of using microminiaturization techniques to produce general purpose computers affordable by many in our society.

Current indications are that more and more capability will be offered at moderate cost and perhaps some decrease in cost. The capabilities currently available for use in homes and schools rival those available in research laboratories just a few short years ago. Some of the more interesting possibilities include:

1. Automatic control of the home environment
2. Home-based educational activities
3. Home experimentation with ideas previously available only in advanced laboratories
4. Access to information bases such as Dow-Jones, medical data bases, weather information bases, and information inquiry bases
5. Home-based work activities (initially for handicapped workers but eventually for many others)
6. The ability to communicate with anyone through a nationwide network of home computers
7. The ability to review and order goods and services through the home computer
8. The ability to deal more directly and personally with the planning of one's affairs such as estate planning
9. Provision of special capabilities to enhance learning opportunities for the handicapped
10. The ability to simulate events and processes
11. The ability to create one's own data bases—for example, to keep track of interesting articles, to keep a home inventory for insurance purposes, and to keep track of one's monthly budget data.

These possibilities just scratch the surface of the potential represented in bringing the computer into the home and school.

1

With special accessories the computer can now draw elaborate colored images (including animated images); speak using vocabularies limited only by the computer's storage space; listen to and "understand" up to 64 words; play and create multivoice musical compositions; and provide sophisticated capabilities for typing, editing, and formatting letters and documents. With a home computer one can control and operate a robot, control other mechanical devices such as furnaces and humidifiers, and create special character sets in order to learn other languages. With a digital tablet one can recreate a drawing and then modify it using a "drawing editor" program. With a digital plotter one can draw in color on paper for use in papers, books, or as general artwork.

In the past several years the list price of the average "neat" child's toy has increased from about $9.95 to about $49.95. With that shift in price and the advent of microminiaturized electronic circuits, one may readily find toys that talk with small but interesting vocabularies. Examples are talking calculators and spelling games. The interest of children in robots has spawned a whole new area of children's toys ranging from radio controlled race cars to small robots complete with microcomputer control units which can be programed to do various things.

Even the old standby mechanical devices—stove, washer, dryer, automobile, etc.—are now fair prey to the engineers who want to use microcomputers to simplify things and at the same time give products greater capability. As it turns out, using a microcomputer also frequently reduces costs.

What Is a Microcomputer?

Now that is really a knotty question! At one time it meant a very small computer of very limited capability. Today, a small computer frequently has more power and usefulness than some medium-sized computers of just a few years ago.

Frequently the term *microcomputer* refers to a computer that costs roughly $300 to $6,000. In addition, the major computational capabilities are concentrated in one electronic component called a "chip." Generally, a microcomputer can not only do computations but can also communicate with terminals and store relatively large quantities of data. Memory on a microcomputer usually ranges from 4K (enough space to store about 4,000 characters) to about 64K (about 64,000 characters). Newer versions of microcomputer chips can control (or address) up to several million memory locations (or characters).

Microcomputers were popularized through kit manufacturers over a period of some 4 years. Now many of the kit manufacturers are disappearing from the scene—either quitting the business or making only fully assembled computers. Naturally in some cases prices have gone up (frequently so has quality and performance). Several large manufacturing and retailing organizations have entered the marketplace with what are termed "appliance" computers. These computers generally are complete basic computers in one package with possibly one to three plug-in units (video screen, tape recorder, or keyboard). The price ranges from $300 to about $1,600 depending on the extra features built in. In all cases, a high level English-like programing language (usually BASIC) is included in permanent memory (Read Only Memory, called ROM). The regular user memory in a microcomputer (Random Access Memory, or RAM) will lose its contents when the computer is turned off. The ROM memory (permanent memory) makes the high level language available when the computer is turned on.

The fundamental functions of the major parts of the "appliance" computer are:

- **Memory**—allows you to temporarily store and use programs and data.
- **Keyboard**—allows you to
  —enter programs
  —enter data
  —enter data under control of a program.
- **Microprocessor**—carries out the instructions contained in the program.
- **Videoscreen**—allows you to see the results of programs.
- **Cassette recorder**—allows you to
  —save programs and/or data from computer memory for later reuse
  —reload programs and/or data into the computer's memory for reuse.

Let's take a more in-depth look at the internal composition of a computer. A computer in general has:

- A central processing unit—a device which performs the fundamental computations.
- A device or devices (clock) which determine the communication sequences or orders within the computer.
- A "bus"—a set of plugs or receptacles into which extra devices may be installed in order to provide extra capability.
- Memory

—Random access memory (RAM) and
—Read only memory (ROM).
- Interface(s)
  —*Terminal interface* allows the computer to communicate with a videoscreen and keyboard.
  —*Cassette interface* allows the computer to store programs and data on audiocassette for later reloading into the computer for reuse.
  —*Disk interface* (frequently called a "controller") provides the capability to store and retrieve programs and data very quickly and allows access to any other piece of data.
  —*Real world control interface(s)* allows control of furnaces, thermostats, burglar alarms, robots, etc.
  —*Special speech interfaces* allow the computer to talk and to "understand" some human speech.
  —*Printer interface* allows the computer to provide relatively complete control of a printing device in order to list programs and print results programs.
- **Power supply**—provides all the power needed to operate the main portion of the computer. Frequently devices added to the computer (e.g. , disk systems and printers) are required to have separate power supplies usually built into the accessory.

With the advent of the appliance or home computer, the definition of what is in a computer varies from manufacturer to manufacturer.

The following diagrams represent graphically each of two general configurations of appliance microcomputers. Figure 1 shows a self-contained appliance microcomputer. In this type of configuration the "interfaces," which allow the microcomputer to control the accessories, plug directly into the keyboard microcomputer package. Figure 2 shows an appliance microcomputer that requires an "expansion box." The interfaces controlling the accessories are plugged into the expansion box in this configuration.

The possibility of home or personal computers became an economic reality when the capability of recording computer data on audiocassettes was developed. Audiocassettes are inexpensive and many people already own cassette recorders of sufficient quality for use on home computers. Audiocassettes designated C-60 (30 minutes per side) can typically hold more than 100,000 characters of data. It can, however, take from 5 to 20 minutes to record or play back a substantial-sized program. In a classroom, that amount of

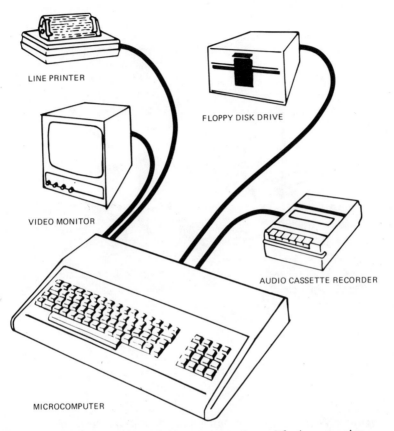

LINE PRINTER

FLOPPY DISK DRIVE

VIDEO MONITOR

AUDIO CASSETTE RECORDER

MICROCOMPUTER

Figure 1. "Self-Contained" Microcomputer with Accessories

time to load a program can severely restrict the number of different programs that can be used in a class period. The cost, though, is obviously minimal. With audiocassettes one cannot get a particular piece of data from the tape without "reading" all preceding pieces of data; in other words, one cannot randomly access data on a low-cost home version of the audiocassette recorder.

The most cost-effective high speed random access data device currently available is the "floppy disk." The floppy disk is also called the floppy diskette. One size floppy diskette is 5¼" and resembles a 45 RPM record; it is very thin (hence floppy) and has two sides coated with a magnetic oxide surface similar to audiotape. Data are recorded in concentric circles or paths (from 35 to 77 depending on the diskette size—5¼" or 8"). Small diskettes may

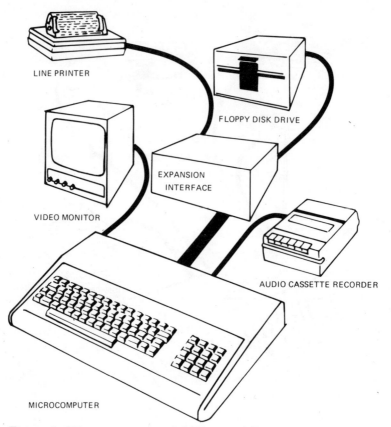

LINE PRINTER

FLOPPY DISK DRIVE

EXPANSION INTERFACE

VIDEO MONITOR

AUDIO CASSETTE RECORDER

MICROCOMPUTER

Figure 2. Microcomputer with External Expansion for Accessories

hold from 50,000 to in excess of 300,000 characters of data on just one side. If a disk drive (the mechanical device used to record or play the diskette) can record or play both sides or surfaces of the diskette, the numbers of course double. A large program which would take 5 to 20 minutes to load from cassette tape would typically load from diskette in about 5 to 30 seconds and any program on the diskette could be found and loaded in about the same amount of time. That would effectively allow a teacher to demonstrate a fair number of programs in one class period. The diskettes range in cost from roughly $5 to $8 a piece in single quantities and the disk drives range in cost from about $400 to $2,600 depending on size and the computer on which they would be used. Some kinds of programs are maximally effective only when used on disk-based microcomputers. For example, equipment inventory systems, equipment scheduling systems, computer-managed instruction systems, and information retrieval systems in general would require the use of at least one floppy disk drive and frequently are much more useful with two drives.

What Is a Program?

The computer is essentially a device with no brains. It has a built-in set of actions which it can carry out, and requires a list of instructions in order to perform a useful task. Each instruction on the list may require the computer to perform one or more of its built-in actions. If the list of instructions contains a mistake then the computer will generally blindly make the mistake. Such a list of instructions is called a program.

The set of instructions a computer can understand is called "machine language." Unfortunately, machine language is not very easily readable by a human. All programs are ultimately interpreted by the computer as machine language. It follows, then, that some programs are not necessarily written directly in machine language; in fact, most are not. Most programs are actually prepared in either "assembly language" or a "high level" language and then automatically translated by the computer into a machine language version which the computer can perform.

The range of programs which can be written may be characterized as follows:

Machine language—the fundamental built-in set of actions for a particular computer not easily learned by users.

Assembly language—a simple language people can understand, used for preparing a list of instructions for the computer. It is itself a program and it gives the user the ability to write a simplified list of instructions (a program) which is subsequently translated into a program made up of machine language versions of the instructions. Assembly language is somewhat difficult to learn.

High level languages (e.g., BASIC, PASCAL, FORTRAN, COBOL, etc.)—an English-like language designed to make it relatively convenient for a person to prepare a list of instructions for a computer. It gives the user the ability to prepare a very easily understood list of instructions (a program) which is subsequently translated into a machine language version. High level languages are generaly much easier to use.

User programs—lists of instructions which are then translated by another program (an assembler or high level language) into a machine language version.

The next chapter will explore the general availability of languages on microcomputers.

CHAPTER 2

Computer Languages for Microcomputers

Computer languages are generally written in one or more of three basic forms: (1) as an interpreter, (2) as a compiler, (3) as a semicompiler.

A language implemented as an interpreter is usually very convenient to use. At one moment one may be constructing a program and in the very next instant actually executing the program. This allows very quick development of programs. The disadvantage of an interpreter is that a considerable part of memory is required for the interpreter and it is needed for both program construction and execution of the finished program. Very often an interpreter will require 8K to 24K of memory space (remember K means thousand).

Appliance computers usually are designed with a particular language built in (that is, permanently available in read-only memory—ROM). Some appliance computers allow the user to "conveniently" change the language by changing the ROM (notably the Apple II and the Sorcerer). The commonly available language is BASIC in ROM and it is in the form of an interpreter. Presumably this was done to make the language maximally easy to use.

Other languages may be called into use from cassette tape or diskette. These languages will be used in the random access memory (RAM). While this procedure is convenient and useful, it reduces the amount of random access memory available to hold a program written in that language. Such a language may be an interpreter, a compiler, or a semicompiler. Now let's move on to compilers.

A language implemented as a compiler is definitely less convenient to use. One uses a program called an editor to create a program file (a list of instructions). The compiler is then invoked to convert the program file into executable machine instructions. A "run-time" package is then used to execute and support your program. A "run-time" package is a set of small programs attached automatically by the computer to your program. They perform special functions with respect to the compiler language. If an error

9

is found when the program has finished running, the entire process is repeated in order to correct the error. As you can see, it is not a really convenient arrangement, but compiler languages frequently make up for inconvenience by being more powerful. An advantage is the fact that "run-time" packages typically run 2K to 8K in size, a significant reduction in memory consumption. This means that larger programs can be constructed and used. Another major advantage is that compiled programs are generally orders of magnitude faster in execution.

A semicompiled language requires the same arrangement as compilers to develop a program. Because this form of language is not a true compiler, the resulting program frequently executes in about the same amount of time as required by a good interpreter. The advantage is in memory space saving. Semicompilers use about the same space as compilers and also use a "run-time" package.

A language is generally chosen on the basis of one or more of these concerns:
• cost and availability
• convenience in program development
• special programming features
• speed of execution
• size of programs which can be developed and
• availability of existing programs written in the language.

It should be noted that in the case of "appliance" computers, the choice may be de facto—that is, a language (usually BASIC) may be built in. With most of the appliance computers, one may choose to use another language or languages.

Another very useful large program is called the disk operating system (DOS). It usually allows one to control and effectively use the disk drives through simple commands. Usually languages which can store and retrieve programs through the disk operating system are available. Frequently the languages allow retrieval of data on a random access basis. That is to say, a program could retrieve any piece of data from disk as rapidly as any other piece of data. Such a procedure is in sharp contrast to sequential access to data where you have to read through a number of pieces of data until you find the one you want. Random access to data would be extremely useful in inventory control programs, information retrieval programs, and scheduling programs, to name just a few.

Now let's take a look at what is generally available for several of the appliance computers in wide use.

APPLE II

The Apple II microcomputer uses the 6502 processor chip as its central processor unit (CPU).

The Apple II has available a mini-assembler in ROM. Two rather more complete and sophisticated programs—a text editor and an assembler—are available from sources outside the Apple company.

The Apple II has been supplied with Integer BASIC in ROM although currently it may be obtained with the floating point BASIC called Applesoft (also in ROM). Applesoft BASIC is available on cassette, diskette, and (as indicated above) in ROM. Of the two BASICS, the Applesoft BASIC is more flexible and potentially more useful. The Applesoft BASIC is more compatible with the BASIC programs published in the microcomputer magazines and journals.

PASCAL is available for the Apple II from Apple and requires 48K of memory and one or more disk drives. The version of PASCAL offered is the University of California San Diego (UCSD) PASCAL. Use of the PASCAL language on the Apple is not as easy or convenient as using BASIC but there are some applications for which PASCAL is more suited than BASIC. The Apple PASCAL provides its own disk operating system as part of PASCAL.

An independent software producer currently offers a computer-assisted instruction language called APPLEPILOT (a version of common PILOT) for use with cassette or diskette.

Another software company offers the language FORTH in a restricted version for the Apple. FORTH is a language which would probably be most useful in a class on programing.

The list processing language called LISP is offered by an independent software company for the Apple II. Again, LISP would probably be most useful in special problems dealing with language manipulation or in a class on programing.

The manufacturers of the Apple II provide their own disk operating system called DOS 3.2. The Applesoft BASIC and the disk operating system were written by two different organizations and consequently the resulting combination can be somewhat inconvenient to use.

One independent software producer does offer modifications to the Apple disk operating system and a special disk controller interface which allows the Apple II to access files stored on a CP/M diskette. This would tend to be useful mostly for text-oriented files or BASIC program files.

Another independent software group offers a completely new disk operating system, file manager, BASIC editor, and assembler for the Apple II. It appears that the system may be more convenient to use—that is, easier to learn and use on a day-to-day basis. This disk operating system is most useful with 48K of memory and of course requires a disk drive.

One of the major software companies, Microsoft, has developed an excellent line of BASIC interpreters and compilers, FORTRAN compiler, COBOL, and an assembly language system for use on Z-80 based systems. Alas, the Apple II is 6502 based. Microsoft has announced availability of the Z-80 SOFTCARD which plugs into the Apple II and can then operate as a Z-80 machine or a 6502 machine. Microsoft also supplies a modified CP/M disk operating system, two BASIC interpreters (one has built-in color graphics commands), and a set of special utility programs. This CP/M system *cannot* read programs or data from other CP/M disks. The utility programs allow transfer of programs from the Apple II CP/M to other CP/M-oriented computers through RS-232-C interfaces and a cable.

TRS-80 (Level I and Level II)

The TRS-80 microcomputer uses the Z-80 processor chip as its central processor unit (CPU).

Radio Shack, a division of Tandy Corporation (manufacturer of the TRS-80), offers a cassette-oriented editor and assembler. The editor and assembler are useful but until recently were not available for use with the disk system. At least two software companies offer modifications for the TRS-80 EDITOR/ASSEMBLER which allow its use with the disk system.

The TRS-80 offers two levels of BASIC. Level I BASIC is an integer BASIC and comes built in on the least expensive machine. Level II BASIC is a floating point BASIC with most of the desirable features of an extended BASIC. The difference between an integer BASIC and a floating point BASIC is in the ability to handle large numbers and the accuracy of manipulating numbers. Floating point BASIC is the most useful in this regard. When level II BASIC is used with the disk operating system, it becomes a user-convenient language with a comprehensive set of features. The manuals provided by Radio Shack for their BASIC languages could well be used as a standard for user manuals in general.

One independent software company offers a cassette-oriented Level III BASIC for the TRS-80 which provides most of the extended features of the TRS-80 disk BASIC and provides some very nice graphics commands. It is used only with a cassette system and was designed by the same software company that prepared the TRS-80 Level II BASIC for Radio Shack.

A computer-assisted instruction language (PILOT) is available in both a cassette and a diskette version for the TRS-80 from an independent software producer.

A version of MUMPS language is being prepared for use in the CP/M disk operating system and should be available then for the TRS-80. The MUMPS language is a very flexible computer-assisted instruction language which was developed originally in the medical field. It has been expanded and now represents a good alternative language for computer-assisted instruction purposes.

A small version of the language FORTH is available in both cassette and diskette format for the TRS-80 from an independent software company.

The language C (a Bell laboratories development) has been produced in a limited feature version for use on the TRS-80. Some of the features of C implemented in TINY C do not follow the normal conventions. The primary use for TINY C would be the teaching of programing languages. The documentation manuals are superb.

A limited-feature version of PASCAL called TINY PASCAL is also available for the TRS-80. The primary use of TINY PASCAL is for teaching programing and experimenting with extending and modifying TINY PASCAL. This version is supplied in a form that allows one to recompile the language and thus extend its capabilities.

Both TINY C and TINY PASCAL are designed to be used with the TRS-80 disk system.

A comprehensive version of FORTRAN compatible with FORTRAN IV is available for use on the TRS-80 disk operating system. Companion programs available include a linking loader, an editor, and a macro-assembler. FORTRAN and the linking loader are available from Radio Shack.

The TRS-80 has a very useful disk operating system which was designed to work conveniently with the language BASIC. In fact, when you get TRS-80 DOS you also get increased BASIC language capability.

All of the above disk-oriented languages are based upon the

TRS-80 disk operating system (TRS-DOS). A widely used disk operating system called CP/M is available in a special version (nonstandard) of CP/M for use on the TRS-80. It requires no physical modifications to the TRS-80 system. A number of editors, assemblers, text or word processors, and languages have been adapted for use with this version of CP/M. It should be noted that not all programs available for CP/M will run on the nonstandard version. Be sure to check before purchase.

Standard CP/M can be used on a TRS-80 if one installs modifications offered by either of two independent companies. Such modifications typically void the Radio Shack warranty. It should be noted that availability of standard CP/M for use does allow use of most of the materials available both from users' groups and/or from commercial firms.

CP/M, at least in the nonstandard version, is available through several independent software brokers. If one has CP/M available, a whole world of languages and applications programs can be acquired and put to use.

The UCSD version of PASCAL is available for use on the TRS-80. It requires 48K of memory and is most useful with two-disk drives. It provides its own disk operating system. The UCSD PASCAL is considered to have a very useful set of features generally considered important to PASCAL. Some minor bugs (errors or problems) have been reported. It is possible to program around the problems.

A version of the language PASCAL is offered which operates in the CP/M disk operating system. This version of PASCAL is relatively complete. For those who want to provide instruction in computer programing, PASCAL is a must for two reasons: PASCAL is becoming a widely used language and PASCAL can also be used to teach aspects of compiler writing (that is, other languages may be created in PASCAL). The CP/M version of PASCAL (not to be confused with the UCSD PASCAL) is very fast in comparison to the UCSD PASCAL.

A comprehensive version of FORTRAN for CP/M is also offered. FORTRAN would probably be most useful for those who want to teach programing or who learned to program in FORTRAN. There are a fair number of programs written in FORTRAN that can be adapted very handily to operate on a microcomputer.

Another version of the language C has been released for the TRS-80 and is designed to operate in a CP/M disk operating system. It was implemented as a compiler. While this C compiler is not as complete as the BELL laboratories version, it is quite respectable.

A complete version of C for CP/M has also been developed. It also is implemented as a compiler and is excellent. It does, however, take 60K of memory and as such will not operate on a TRS-80 system unless major modifications are made to the TRS-80. An adapter kit is available from an independent company for such modification.

The company that created Level II BASIC also offers an excellent extended BASIC compiler for use in CP/M.

A very nice business version of BASIC names CBASIC2 is also offered for the CP/M disk operating system. CBASIC2 is a semi-compiler and thus runs somewhat slower in final execution of a program.

One of the most well-known business languages for computers is COBOL. Versions of COBOL are currently available for use on the CP/M disk operating system. The main uses for COBOL on a microcomputer would be to teach programing and to use existing COBOL programs.

The standard CP/M system includes both a text editor (ED) and an assembler. A limitation of the assembler is that it generates 8080 code rather than Z-80 machine code. The documentation for CP/M and ED needs considerable revision to make it easy to use. Once CP/M and ED are mastered the power made available is impressive.

SORCERER (by Exidy)

The SORCERER microcomputer uses the Z-80 processor chip as its central processor unit.

The disk system normally recommended by Exidy for use on the SORCERER is the MICROPOLIS. The company which produces the MICROPOLIS disk systems offers a disk operating system called MDOS, an extended BASIC (interpreter), an assembler, and an editor. The extended BASIC was produced by Microsoft, a major software producer for microcomputers. This BASIC is *not* totally compatible with other Microsoft BASICS.

The CP/M disk operating system is available for use on the SORCERER in either small (5 1/4″) or large (8″) disk format. With the ability to use CP/M comes the availability of such languages as FORTRAN, PASCAL, ALGOL, COBOL, and a variety of

BASICS—both compilers and interpreters. Almost all of the programs available under CP/M will run on a SORCERER with CP/M. Effective use of CP/M requires about 48K of memory and two disk drives.

The SORCERER is very attractive for word processing because it offers upper and lower case and shows 30 lines x 64 characters per line. A variety of word processor programs is available under the CP/M disk operating system.

OHIO SCIENTIFIC (OSI)

This manufacturer has several lines of microcomputers. The model offered in the same class as TRS-80, APPLE, SORCERER, and PET is called C4P; the disk version is called the C4P MF. Both models feature the use of the 6502 microprocessor chip.

The BASIC available in these two models is a Microsoft BASIC with nine digits of precision; it is one of the fastest interpreters currently implemented on microcomputers.

The C4P MF offers a basic disk operating system and has available an editor and assembler. Because the C4P MF does not use the Z-80 or 8080 computer chips, CP/M is not available.

Ohio Scientific does market a line called the Challenger III series. The Challenger III series has three microcomputer chips in each computer, thus allowing the use of a wide range of software. The three processor chips are the 6502, the 6800, and the Z-80. As one might expect, the Challenger III disk system can indeed use CP/M. OSI can provide CP/M, an editor, assembler, Microsoft BASIC (interpreters), FORTRAN compiler, and COBOL. The availability of CP/M for the Challenger III series makes it possible to use most of the generally available software prepared for use under the CP/M disk operating system.

CBM/PET (commodore)

The CBM/PET microcomputer uses the 6502 processor chip as its central processor unit.

Commodore Business Machines manufactures the PET microcomputer. It contains a ROM BASIC (8K) by Microsoft.

Several independent software companies offer assembler/editor systems oriented toward cassette tape.

One company offers a macro-assembler/editor system on either cassette tape or disk for the PET.

PETFORTH, a stack-oriented compiler language, is offered independently for PETs with cassette drives. The CBM/PET disk system comes with a disk operating system (DOS) and its own disk BASIC.

ATARI 800

The ATARI 800 microcomputer uses the 6502 processor chip as its central processor unit.

The ATARI 800 comes with ROM BASIC containing color graphics commands.

ATARI also offers a disk drive with a disk operating system and a disk BASIC.

Figure 3. Texas Instruments TI 99/4 Microcomputer

TI 99/4 (Texas Instrument)

The TI 99/4 microcomputer is the only currently produced appliance microcomputer based upon a 16 bit processor chip (the TMS 9900).

Currently no assembler/editor systems have been released.

The Texas Instrument folks have been demonstrating a disk system and disk BASIC of late.

Figure 4. Texas Instruments TI 99/4 Microcomputer Disk System

Figure 5. Inserting a Program Cartridge into a Texas Instruments TI 99/4 Microcomputer

CHAPTER 3

Disk Operating Systems and What They Can Do For You

Disk systems, though more expensive than cassette, offer two major advantages:
- Programs and data files can be rapidly loaded into BASIC. Programs and data can also be saved rapidly.
- They allow you to create and use both random access data files.

The question of speed can be illustrated by pointing out that large programs frequently take 5 to 10 minutes to load from cassette into BASIC. This means that a teacher cannot effectively demonstrate very many different programs in a period. This can be more of a problem when you need to first load another language from cassette (5 to 15 minutes) and then a program for that language (another 5 to 10 minutes). Loading those programs and languages from a disk usually takes less than 30 to 40 seconds.

Random access to any piece of information recorded on a cassette is not currently possible in appliance computers. Random access becomes very important in student record keeping systems, computer-assisted instruction systems, information retrieval systems, inventory systems, and other large file systems.

The four disk systems for which information is readily available are TRS-80 Model I-TRSDOS; Apple II DOS; CBM/PET DOS, and CP/M based disk systems. Let's take a look at some of the features and commands available.

TRS-80 Model I-TRSDOS

The disk operating system itself has as some of its commands the following:

Command	Action
BASIC	brings the language BASIC into operation
BASIC *	returns from TRSDOS into BASIC, preserving any BASIC program previously in memory

AUTO filename	sets up the disk so that when the machine is first turned on it starts executing the specified program
CLOCK ON/OFF	specified program displays the internal clock (shows elapsed time since starting OR current time of day)
TIME	sets the internal clock to start timing from the time specified
DATE	sets the specified date internally in the system
BACKUP	copies the entire disk onto another disk
FORMAT	initializes the disk to accept files for storage
VERIFY ON/OFF	activates or de-activates automatic validity check of disk recording operations
COPY	copy individual files from disk-to-disk or to different name on same disk
DIR	lists all user programs on the disk on the video display
KILL	deletes a disk file or program
FREE	determines space left on disk
LIST	displays text file on video screen
LOAD	loads a machine language program into memory
PRINT	prints text file on printer
RENAME	allows you to rename a disk file

BASIC allows some disk commands to be used from BASIC programs:

Command	Action
LOAD	brings program into BASIC
SAVE	saves current BASIC program to disk
KILL	deletes specified program from disk
MERGE	gets specified program from disk and loads it over existing program in memory
RUN	gets program from disk and executes it
OPEN	sets up file for data activity
CLOSE	inactivates data file
FIELD	specifies how you want data stored in random access files
GET	gets data specified from disk record specified (random access)
INPUT #	gets data from a sequential data file

PRINT #   saves data to a sequential data file

TRS-80 DOS does not at this time allow you to display a disk directory directly in BASIC

TRS-80 DOS and BASIC is very similar to the disk BASIC used on the large DEC minicomputers used in colleges and universities.

APPLE II—DOS 3.2

The disk operating system commands on the APPLE II are available from BASIC. Some of the commands are:

Command	Action
INIT	initialize a disk to accept files
LOAD	load a machine language program or data into memory
SAVE	save an area of memory to disk
RUN	execute machine language program from disk
CATALOG	display names of files on disk
RENAME	rename files
DELETE	"remove" a file from disk
LOCK	write protect a file
UNLOCK	remove write protect from a file
VERIFY	check a file to see if it is still good
OPEN	set up file to accept data
CLOSE	deactivate data file
WRITE	save data-to-data file
READ	get data from data file
SAVE	save a BASIC program to disk
LOAD	get a BASIC program from disk
RUN	execute a BASIC program

The random access disk procedures are unlike any other disk system and require you to keep track of your procedures carefully. The procedure for using the disk system for data files from BASIC represents features added on to the BASIC. As a result developing your own data file programs on the APPLE II requires some extra effort.

CBM/PET DOS

The disk operating system commands for the CBM/PET are:

Command	Action
VALIDATE	initialize disk to accept files
DUPLICATE	copy one disk to another
RENAME	rename files
SCRATCH	erase a file

The disk commands available in BASIC are:

Command	Action
LOAD	get BASIC program from disk
SAVE	save BASIC program to disk
VERIFY	compare program on disk to program in memory
PRINT #	execute a string containing a special DOS command
OPEN	set up data file to accept date
CLOSE	deactivate data file

To display a disk directory in a CBM/PET disk BASIC system:
READY
LOAD "∅", 8 CR
SEARCHING FOR ∅
LOADING
READY
LIST CR

Random access data files in CBM/PET disk BASIC system require the use of some substantial subroutines to be added to each BASIC program using random access data files. This is not a trivial task.

CP/M DISK OPERATING SYSTEM

The disk operating system commands for CP/M are:

Command	Action
ERA	erase a file
DIR	display the disk directory
REN	rename a file
SAVE	save a block of memory to disk
TYPE	display text file on the video display
STAT	show the remaining available amount of disk space

LOAD   change á machine language file into a
                        direct executing program
SYSGEN   prepare disk to hold a CP/M system
SUBMIT   execute a file of DOS commands
PIP   allows you to send or get files to or from
                        any input/output device; e.g., video,
                        printer, keyboard, disk, etc.

CP/M is a very powerful disk operating system.

BASIC disk commands depend on those available in the BASIC you chose to use.

CHAPTER 4

What's in a Microcomputer System?

The major purpose of this chapter is to examine the "big" four microcomputer systems—Apple II, CBM/PET, Sorcerer, and TRS-80—to see what their capabilities are and to define two levels of system: an excellent educator's system and an absolute "bare bones" system. Since costs vary over time and from bid to bid, no prices are quoted. You should be able to use this information to compare costs and shop for the capabilities you want.

Before you make a final decision in purchasing a system, carefully:

- analyze the tasks you wish to use it for,
- examine the availability of the kinds of programs you will want to use.

A computer without appropriate software means you will have to do a great deal of programing yourself.

Apple II

The Apple II in its most fundamental form contains a keyboard unit. The keyboard unit contains:

- 6502 microprocessor unit
- 16K of RAM for programs
- a cassette interface used to transfer programs to and from cassettes at about 150 characters a second
- a video generator capable of
    A. 40 characters per line by 24 lines per screen
    B. color graphics mode of
        1. 40 x 48 dots and 15 colors
        2. 280 x 192 dots and 6 colors
- plug-ins for eight accessories
- game paddle plug-in.

Note: No video display or cassette recorder is included.

Note: The Apple II may be used with a home TV by adding a video modulator.

24

The fundamental unit may be expanded significantly. You can:
- add up to 32K RAM in the keyboard unit
- add printer interface to plug into keyboard and then add printer
- add Disk II interface to plug into keyboard unit and a disk drive (a disk controller controls up to two drives)
- add telephone coupler (modem) to communicate with other similarly equipped computers
- add RS-232-C interface
- add graphics tablet to create or trace drawings and transfer them to the video display
- add clock/calendar card
- add color monitor or video display.

An excellent educator's system would include:
- a 32K Apple II or Apple II PLUS
- a color monitor
- a Disk II single disk system (two disk drives preferred)
- a printer.

From outside manufacturers you should consider obtaining a light pen. See chapter 5 for other accessories.

An absolute "bare bones" system would include:
- a 16K Apple II or Apple II PLUS
- a black-and-white video monitor
- a cassette recorder.

CBM/PET (by Commodore)

The CBM/PET in its most fundamental form contains one unit. The CBM/PET unit provides:
- a 6502 microprocessor
- 8K of RAM
- the IEEE expansion bus
- either a calculator style keyboard or a full size keyboard
- a 9″ black-and-white video monitor
- a video generator capable of:
  40 characters per line and 25 lines per screen and
  a very interesting set of graphics characters
- a built-in cassette recorder (*not* a normal cassette recorder) if you get the calculator style keyboard.

Figure 6. Commodore CBM/PET Microcomputer

The fundamental unit may be expanded significantly as follows:
- add up to 32 RAM to the original unit (internally)
- add a printer
- add a dual disk drive system
- add a telephone coupler (modem)
- add a voice synthesizer
- add a cassette drive.

An excellent educator system would include:
- 32K CBM/PET with full-size keyboard
- a printer
- a dual disk system (it is offered only in dual disk arrangement).

Figure 7. Commodore CBM/PET Printer

Figure 8. Commodore CBM/PET Disk System

An absolute "bare bones" system would include:
- a 16K CBM/PET with full size keyboard
- a PET cassette recorder.

SORCERER (by Exidy)

The Sorcerer's most fundamental unit contains a keyboard unit. The keyboard unit contains:

- a Z-80 micro-processor
- 16K RAM
- a dual cassette interface capable of recording programs at 30 characters a second or 120 characters a second
- a video generator capable of
  - A. 64 character lines and 30 lines per screen
  - B. 64 predefined graphics characters
  - C. 64 user-definable graphics characters
  - D. effective graphics resolution of 512 x 240 dots
- a RS-232-C interface
- a printer interface
- a place to plug in a ROM (read only memory) package.

Note: No cassette recorder is supplied but a reasonable quality audio recorder should work well.

Note: No video display is provided. You must use a good quality video monitor, e.g. a Leedex 100.

The fundamental unit may be expanded significantly as follows:

- expand the keyboard memory to 48K RAM
- add an expansion interface
- add a disk controller interface and a disk drive
- add a printer with parallel "Centronics" interface capability.

An excellent educators system would include:

- an 32K Sorcerer
- a black-and-white video display
- an expansion interface
- a disk controller interface and a disk drive (preferably two disk drives)
- the CP/M disk operating system with microsoft Disk Basic.

An absolute "bare bones" system would include:
- a 16K Sorcerer
- a black and white video display
- a good quality audiocassette recorder.

Figure 9. Exidy SORCERER Microcomputer

Figure 10. Exidy SORCERER Video Display and Disk System

Figure 11. Radio Shack TRS-80 Level II Microcomputer

TRS-80 Model I Level II (Radio Shack)

The TRS-80 Model I Level II microcomputer in its most fundamental form consists of three units:
- keyboard unit containing
  A. Z-80 micro-processor
  B. 4K of random access memory for use with programs expandable to 16K RAM in the keyboard unit
  C. cassette interface capable of transferring programs at a rate of about 50 characters a second
  D. a video display generator capable of
    1. 64 character lines and 16 lines per screen
    2. graphics of 48 x 128 dot resolution
- black-and-white video display
- audiocassette tape recorder.

The fundamental unit may be expanded significantly as follows:
- expand keyboard to 16K RAM
- add printer to use with the basic keyboard unit
- add expansion interface which is also capable of holding an additional 32K RAM. The additional RAM may be added in 16K increments. This unit also provides:

Figure 12. Radio Shack TRS-80 Level I Microcomputer

Figure 13. Radio Shack TRS-80 Level II Microcomputer with Disk System, Expansion Interface, and Printer

    A. control of dual-cassette tape recorders
    B. a printer controller interface
    C. a disk controller interface
    D. a real time clock
- add one or more disk drives (up to four)
- add RS-232-C interface to expansion interface
- add telephone coupler (modem) to expansion interface and RS-232-C interface to dial up time-shared systems or other TRS-80 systems
- add speech synthesizer to phonetically generate speech by computer
- add voice recognition unit to allow the computer to respond to oral command.

An excellent educators system would include:
- the 16K Model I Level II TRS-80
- the expansion interface with 16K of memory
- a printer
- one disk drive (preferably two).

From outside manufacturers you should probably consider adding a light pen. See chapter 5 for other accessories.

An absolute "bare bones" educator system would be the 16K Model I Level II TRS-80.

CHAPTER 5

Special Accessories: State of the Art

The appliance microcomputer is a complete general purpose computer in its own right. It generally comes equipped to allow both computing and game playing. But, because you have complete control of your microcomputer—i.e., you don't time-share it with someone else simultaneously—you can actually engage in many activities found only in research laboratories just 2 to 5 years ago.

For example, you can equip your microcomputer to listen for verbal commands, speak to you, allow you to convert drawings into video images, control robots, convert videocamera information into computer information, read and mark sense cards inexpensively, communicate via telephone lines with other computers, and store and retrieve around 10 to 16 million characters or bytes of data on a disk drive.

The microcomputer is rapidly becoming an indispensable tool, an important part of the home entertainment world and a means of allowing people to expand their learning horizons.

The microcomputer influence will become so pervasive within 5 to 7 years that computer literacy will become a prime job requirement. The range of accessories for microcomputers will play no small part in the development of computer literacy.

This chapter surveys the purchasable and hence usable state of the art accessories currently available for appliance microcomputers.

The accessories surveyed include:

Computer furniture

Lower case adapters—to allow the display and typing of lower case letters as well as capital letters.

Lower case and graphics symbol generator—to allow the display of lower case and special graphics characters.

Real time clock—to allow timing of delay of student response or answer.

Joysticks and paddles—to allow the user to move graphic images around on the screen. Could be used to allow some learning-disabled students to respond without typing.

Video display (text oriented)—to allow the display of more text on the video screen. This is sometimes desirable when doing word processing.

Light pens—to allow users to point a special pen or wand at the surface of a video screen to indicate a response. These are sometimes used to "draw" on the screen and have the computer convert the drawing for storage and later retrieval.

Speech recognition—allows the computer to "understand" a fixed series of words or to convert human speech into computer data.

Voice synthesis—allows the computer to generate speech of varying levels of intelligibility.

Music synthesizer—usually allows the user to enter multipart or voice music in a relatively convenient form into the computer and then have the computer "play" the music in one or more voices. Frequently allows changing of the quality of voice.

Graphics tablets (digitizers)—allow tracing or "sketching" drawings and translating them into reproducible computer data. The data may be modified but is viewable later on the videoscreen.

Digital plotters—draw elaborate line drawings on paper. Frequently these draw on a flat surface, but there are one or two which draw on paper curled around a drum.

Electronic typewriter controller—allows you to use your new IBM electronic typewriter as a printing device on your microcomputer.

Print graphics—features a way of modifying a printing terminal to also print graphic images on paper.

Video graphic add-on (high resolution)—allows display of very detailed images on the videoscreen for microcomputers which do not originally have this ability built in.

Digitizing video images—features a way to take the output of a videocamera and convert it into a form usable by a microcomputer. Devices like this make it possible to do things like computer-printed T-shirts.

Real world control—allows you to control the turning on or off of electrical devices, temperature sensing, humidity sensing, or some combination of these, under the control of a program in your microcomputer.

Robots—features both a robot-controlled arm (very lightweight) and a robot turtle which can move in any direction and sense obstacles. Both devices are connected by cable to your microcomputer and controlled by a program.

Card reader (mark sense)—allows you to input test results, experimental data, and even computer programs via mark sense cards to your microcomputer.

High speed cassettes—allows a low-cost alternate to disk drives for program storage and retrieval.

Mass storage ("wafer")—another low-cost alternative to disk drives for program storage and retrieval.

Large floppy disk systems (8-inch)—allow substantial increase (about 3 times the storage space) in disk storage space at moderate cost.

Special expansion interface—to allow the use of mini-floppy disk drives, 8-inch floppy disk drives and the Winchester type hard disk drives.

Hard disk system (nonremovable)—allows storage of 9.6 million characters (bytes) to 18 million characters currently. These are particularly useful for large data bases such as student records.

Hard disk backup system—allows the use of a video cartridge recorder to save all 10 million characters of data in about 10 minutes and replace them in the same amount of time when needed.

Cartridge hard disk system (removable)—allows storage of 5 million characters on a nonremovable drive and 5 million on a removable cartridge, thus allowing you to make and keep backup copies conveniently.

Resource sharing with multiple microcomputers—allows disk drives and printer to be used in common by several microcomputers. The advantage is reduced cost, with some reduced storage space and convenience.

Telephone coupler (modem)—allows convenient use of the telephone to access other computers.

Each of the surveyed accessory areas includes the type of microcomputer with which it will work (where known) and the manufacturer or vendor.

Computer Furniture

CF&A
Computer Furniture and Accessories, Inc.
1441 West 132nd Street
Gardena, CA 90249
213-327-7710

DEVOKE Data Products
3780 Fabian Way
Palo Alto, CA 94303
415-494-8844

GUSDORF Corporation
6900 Manchester
St. Louis, MO 63143

Lowercase Adapters

Don Paymar has introduced a lowercase adapter (LCA) for the Apple II. It displays lowercase with true descenders on the letters and symbols. It is compatible with Apple II DOS and most printers.

Requires—Apple II

Don Paymar
P.O. Box A-133
C.S. 6800
Costa Mesa, CA 92627
714-645-1411

Square Sales has introduced an upper/lowercase TRS-80 modification which provides shift and shiftlock for uppercase and no shift for lowercase. It also displays upper- and lowercase.

Requires—TRS-80 Level II Model I

Square Sales-Service, Inc.
128 Bala Avenue
Bala Cynwyd, PA 19004

Lowercase and Graphic Symbols Generator Kit

For TRS-80 Level II Model I. Creates true descender characters, special symbols, graphics based on thin lines, and textured backgrounds. Includes demonstration programs on cassette.
Requires—Electric pencil type of lowercase hardware modification to your keyboard; requires installation.

G. P. Associates
P.O. Box 22822
Sacramento, CA 95822

Real Time Clocks

Mountain Hardware has developed a real time clock plug-in card for the Apple II with accuracy of 1 millisecond. It allows you to automatically keep track of time and data and time events. It has on-board battery backup to keep the clock running even when the computer is off. This accessory would be useful to time the response of learners in computer-assisted instruction, computer-managed instruction, or instructional simulations and games.

Requires—Apple II

Mountain Hardware
300 Harvey West Blvd.
Santa Cruz, CA 95060

Joysticks and Paddles

A2D Company has released the A2K/Apple II joystick. It features plug-in compatibility, precision open-gimbaled self-centering stick and two game pushbuttons. It comes with a 6' cable and is plug-in compatible with the Apple II.

Requires—Apple II

A2D Company
P.O. Box 6471
Greenville, SC 29606
803-297-0552

Creative Software has developed a joystick interface for the TRS-80 Model I. It plugs into the expansion interface with no changes. Three sockets allow the use of ATARI or Fairchild joysticks.

Requires—TRS-80 Level II, 16K, expansion interface
Creative Software
P.O. Box 4030
Mountain View, CA 94040

A package of two game paddles, interface, speaker, controlling software, power supply, and documentation has been produced for the TRS-80 Model I (Level II). Includes two games on cassette.
Requires—TRS-80 Level II Model I

Electronic Systems
P.O. Box 21638
San Jose, CA 95151
408-448-0800

Video Display (Text oriented)

The DOUBLEVISION video display board for the Apple II
allows the display of 80 characters per line for 24 lines per screen.
The normal Apple II mode is 40 characters and 24 lines. Provides
upper/lowercase, programable cursor, software, shift lock, built-
in light pen capability, and inverse video. Does not allow text and
high resolution graphics on the screen simultaneously.
Requires—Apple II
The Computer Shop
16919 Hawthorne Blvd.
Lawndale, CA 90260
213-371-4010

M & R Enterprises has produced a plug-in card for the Apple II
which gives an 80-character by 24-line video display called SUP-
R-TERMINAL. Use of the card obviates the ability to do high
resolution graphics. It is useful for word processing work. It provides upper- and lowercase and inverse video. You can define your
own character set. A special video balance circuit allows use of the
board with "low cost" 8 MHZ videomonitors. Works with the Apple
II Communications board to allow the Apple II to be an intelligent
terminal for use on time-sharing systems.
Requires—Apple II
M & R ENTERPRISES
P.O. Box 61011
Sunnyvale, CA 94088

Light Pens

The 3G Company has released a light pen for the TRS-80 Model I
microcomputer. Another model has also been released for the
PET.

Available for—TRS-80 Model I; CBM/PET.

ESMARK Inc. has developed a light pen for use with micro-computers which use cassette with the output jack grounded to the computer and a readable single bit input port. In particular, Esmark has released a VIDIET-STIK (light pen) for use with the TRS-80 Model I. Included is a demonstration cassette tape and a calibration program. Two additional sets of programs which use the VIDIET-STIK are available. These programs include LIGHTPEG, ENDRUM (Othello), LIFE 9, LITEGAMMON, STIKWUMPUS and MAZEMASTER.

Requires—TRS-80 Model I, any size and configuration

ESMARK INC.
507½ E. McKinley Hwy.
Mishawaka, IN 46544
219-255-3035

Micro Data Systems is offering a light pen called the Micro Pen II for the TRS-80 Model I. It operates directly through the cassette plug-in on the back of the keyboard rather than through the cassette recorder itself.

Requires—TRS-80 Level II, 16K, Cassette

Micro Data Systems
Dept B
7275 Meath Way
No. Highlands, CA 95660
916-447-7048

Photopoint light pen for TRS-80 includes six programs (three on tape). Complete data on preparing your own program for the light pen. For Radio Shack TRS-80 Level II Model I.

MICRO MATRIX
P.O. Box 938
Pacifica, CA 94044

HIRES light pen for Apple II which allows drawing on screen in both low resolution and high resolution modes. Allows creation of menus, etc. Includes a light pen calculator program and a light pen TIC-TAC-TOE program.

Requires—Apple II, Applesoft ROM and 48K

PROGRESSIVE SOFTWARE
P.O. Box 273
Plymouth Meeting, PA 19462

NEW PEN BASIC (low memory routine to add six commands to LII TRS-80 to control or use the PHOTOPOINT light pen)

MICRO MATRIX
P.O. Box 938
Pacifica, CA 94044
415-355-4635
Available for—TRS-80 Model I Level II.

Symtec has developed a high resolution light pen for use with the Apple II. It has X and Y and sensitivity adjustment, synchronization adjustment for remote source, and a reset touch switch. Software in BASIC is provided. It is also usable with the MUSE PILOT II LANGUAGE.
Available for—Apple II.
SYMTEC Inc.
22223 Telegraph Rd.
Southfield, MI 48072
313-352-1790

Speech Recognition

Heuristics Inc. has introduced a plug-in board for the Apple II which can recognize spoken words and then take a preprogramed action. It comes in two models—one which recognizes up to 32 words and one 64 words. The recognition accuracy is amazing when the background noise level is relatively low. The manual, an education in itself, is really a laboratory manual in speech recognition.
Requires—Apple II
Heuristics, Inc.
900 N. San Antonio Road
Los Altos, CA 94022

"Words or phrases may be used to enter data, control or instruct the TRS-80 without having to type on the keyboard." VOXBOX has a vocabulary of up to 32 words, and the vocabulary and resulting actions can be programed by the user. It has an 85-95% recognition level based upon distinctly pronounced words. Recommended uses are (1) experimentation and (2) entertainment. Includes a machine language controlling program and three demonstration programs. For TRS-80 Level II Model I.

RADIO SHACK
1300 One Tandy Center
Fort Worth, TX 76102

COGNIVOX for the Exidy Sorcerer provides 16-word vocabulary and plugs in to the parallel port. Provides both voice input and output.

VOICETEK
P.O. Box 388
Goleta, CA 93017

Voice Synthesis

Mountain Hardware has developed a plug-in board for the Apple II which allows the Apple to do voice syntheses. It produces high quality humanlike speech under program control. It requires an external amplifier and speaker. SUPERTALKER allows you to speak into its microphone. It then digitizes your spoken words and places the results in RAM. SUPERTALKER also plays back any or all portions to produce humanlike speech.
Requires—Apple II
Mountain Hardware
300 Harvey West Blvd.
Santa Cruz, CA 95060

Radio shack has introduced a voice synthesizer for the TRS-80 Level I and II (Model I). This synthesizer is actually a VOTRAX under the Radio Shack label. It allows speech synthesis using phonetic constructions. Actual implementation in BASIC programs is quite straightforward.

Requires—TRS-80 Model I

RADIO SHACK
700 One Tandy Center
Fort Worth, TX 76102

Two-Way Digital Speech

The SUPERTALKER-SD200, for a two-way input/output speech digitizer, is available from Mountain Hardware. It also features speech compression to allow 100% faster transfer of words and phrases from disk.

Available for—Apple II, 48K, and Disk II.

Mountain Hardware
300 Harvey West Blvd.
Santa Cruz, CA 95060
408-429-8600

Music Synthesizer

The 10-5-16 ALF music synthesizer for the Apple II allows 1 to 9 voice generation in either monaural or stereophonic mode. Provides a complete music generation editor and play program. Shows the music in high resolution graphics as it is played. Provides full piano scale, programable volume, programable envelopes, automatic key signature, automatic measure bars, section repeat, and ability to save music to cassette or disk.

Requires—Apple II

INTEGER BASIC
  WITH DISK 32K
  WITHOUT DISK 24K
APPLESOFT
  WITH DISK 40K
  WITHOUT DISK 32K
ALF PRODUCTS
1448 Estes
Denver, CO 80215

The MICROCOMPOSER music system for the Apple II can produce up to four simultaneous voices, and allows programing of pitch, rhythm, and timbre. Tempo is interactively controlled through a game paddle or joystick. Allows you to compose, edit, play, and save music to cassette or diskette. The voices may be assigned an organ, reed, string, or brass sound individually. No amplifier is required, just a speaker.

Requires—Apple II 16K

MICRO TECHNOLOGY UNLIMITED
841 Galaxy Way
P.O. Box 4596
Manchester, NH 03108
603-627-1464

The MUSIC BOX plugs into the TRS-80 Model I keyboard or expansion interface. It allows you to compose and play music over a seven-octave range, up to four notes simultaneously. Also allows you to create special sound effects from phasors to bells and whistles. Has a volume control, a 400 mw amplifier and a phono-jack. Includes software on cassette.

Requires—Level II Basic and 32K or larger TRS-80

NEWTECH Computer Systems, Inc.
230 Clinton Street
Brooklyn, NY 11201
212-625-6220

Graphics Tablets (Digitizers)

Apple is marketing a graphics tablet for use with the Apple II. It allows tracing of existing artwork or creation of artwork to be converted to high resolution graphics. Over 20 special functions are available by use of the special pen used with the tablet. The drawing area is 10" x 11" and may be software specified as smaller. The system is designed to be convenient and useful.

Requires—Apple II, Applesoft ROM, 48K, Disk II and a color monitor (black-and-white may be used but would not show which colors were being used and total color effect.)

APPLE COMPUTER Inc.
10260 Bandley Drive
Cupertino, CA 95014

Houston Instruments provides a device called the HIPAD digitizer tablet. It has a resolution of 0.005" and a relocatable origin. It accommodates either RS-232-C or a parallel port. It has a digitizing area of 11" x 11" and an accuracy of ±0.015".

Available for—any microcomputer which has a controllable RS-232-C serial port or a controllable parallel port.

Houston Instruments
One Houston Square
Austin, TX 78753
512-837-2820

Summagraphics Corporation offers a data tablet called the BITPAD. It has an accuracy of ±0.004″ and a resolution of 0.005″. It also features a relocatable origin, free cursor and a magnifying cursor.

Summagraphics Corporation
35 Brentwood Avenue
Fairfield, CT 06430
203-384-1344

The VERSAWRITER digitizer drawing board allows you to recreate or create a picture which is then converted into high-resolution graphics on an Apple II. It has an 8 1/2″ x 11″ work area and also allows you to add text to the graphic.

Requires—Apple II, Applesoft ROM, 32K and Disk II

Rainbow Computing
9719 Reseda Blvd.
Northridge, CA 91324

Digital Plotters

Houston Instruments has developed a plotter called the HIPLOT digital plotter. It uses 8 1/2″ x 11″ paper with a plot speed to 2.4″ per second. The resolution is either 0.01″ or 0.005″. It has adjustable baud rate, adjustable step size, setup for serial port, and also setup for parallel port.

Available for—all microcomputers with either a serial RS-232 C port or a controllable parallel port.

Houston Instruments
One Houston Square
Austin, TX 78753
512-837-2820

Strobe, Inc. has designed a low-cost drum plotter for use with the TRS-80, Apple II, Pet, and the Sorcerer. It produces high resolution graphics and interactive coordinate input. Driver programs are available in TRS-80 Level II Basic, Applesoft BASIC,

CBASIC (under CP/M), Microsoft BASIC and Fortran (under CP/M or TRSDOS).
STROBE INC.
897-5AA Independence Ave.
Mountain View, CA 94043
415-969-5130

The MIPLOT intelligent plotter allows one to do X and Y axis plotting of graphics. Allows automatic line generator and character generation. Provides a self-test mode and uses ordinary hard-tip felt pens.

SYSTEMS FORMULATE CORPORATION
39 Town & Country Village
Palo Alto, CA 94301
415-326-9100

Electronic Typewriter Controller

Compusystems has released a controller for use with the new IBM electronic typewriters such as the IBM ET50, ET60, and ET75.

COMPUSYSTEMS
P.O. Box 5144
2301 Devine St.
Columbia, SC 29205
803-254-0804

Print Graphics

Selanar Corporation offers a conversion kit for use on the DEC writer II terminal which allows the DEC writer to become an elaborate graphics plotter. It provides 1320 x 792 dots per page, bidirectional line feed, multiple character sets, multiple interfaces such as RS-232 C compatability, and 40-character-per-second printing speed.

Selanar Corporation
2403 DeLa Cruz Blvd.
Santa Clara, CA 95050
408-727-2811

Video Graphics Add-On

The CAT-100 provides a 256-color imaging system which can digitize a videoframe in 1/16th of a second and store it in its own memory. Resolution is selectable from 256 to 1280 picture elements (PIXELS) per television line. Can display 16 gray levels or 16 colors on black-and-white, RGB, or NTSC color monitors. Has character generator and light pen input.

Available for—TRS-80 and SORCERER.

DIGITAL GRAPHICS SYSTEMS
441 California Avenue
Palo Alto, CA 94306
415-494-6088

This unit provides upper/lowercase, reverse video, blink, 64 x 48 graphics in eight colors or 128 x 192 graphics in four colors or 256 x 192 graphics in one color, allows mixture of text and low resolution graphics on the screen. Includes a cassette of demonstration software.

INTEGRATED SERVICE SYSTEMS, Inc.
1011 West Broadway
Minneapolis, MN 55411
612-522-6631

This accessory designed for the CBM/PET provides 320 x 200 dot high resolution black-and-white graphics. Each dot is individually addressable and allows both text and graphics simultaneously. Has 8K of RAM of its own to support the graphics.

MICRO TECHNOLOGY UNLIMITED
841 Galaxy Way
P.O. Box 4596
Manchester, NH 03108
603-627-1464

The PERCOM ELECTRIC CRAYON provides color graphics for the TRS-80 Level II Model I. It allows a range of graphics from a combined text and low resolution graphics to a high resolution 256 x 192 dot graphics mode and allows up to eight colors depending on the graphics mode chosen, and has its own internal memory. Includes listings of level II Basic programs.

Requires—TRS-80 Level II Model I 16K

PERCOM DATA COMPANY, Inc.
211 N. Kirby
Garland, TX 75042
214-272-3421

Hi Res Graphics

SubLOGIC has developed a high performance graphics display for use with the TRS-80 Model I. The 50/T80 graphics system provides a 256 x 240 dot resolution screen capability. SubLOGIC also has available 2D and 3D graphics projection software packages which are quite powerful. The graphics packages can be driven from BASIC programs.

Requires—TRS-80 Level II, 16 K, Cassette

SubLOGIC
Box V
Savoy, IL 61874
217-359-8482

Digitizing Video Images

Micro Works offers the Model DS-65 DIGISECTOR plug-in card for the Apple II. It represents the first random access video-digitizer for the Apple II. It processes the output of a videocamera into data which the Apple II can store in RAM. Its resolution is 256 x 256 dots with 64 levels of gray scale. It accepts either NTSC interlaced signals or industrial video input signals and scans directly to the high resolution screen mode. The resulting image can be saved to disk and subsequently recalled on demand.

Requires—Apple II, 32K-48K, Disk II and a video camera are recommended.

MICRO WORKS
P.O.Box 1110
Del Mar, CA 92014
714-942-2400

Real World Control

The MICROBOX allows use of an Apple II to switch on and off external AC devices such as relays, motors, lights, and solenoids. Controls four AC outlets up to 200 watts each. Light emitting devices (LED's) indicate the off/on status of each outlet.

CJM Industries, Dept MB
316B Victory Drive
Herndon Industrial Park
Herndon, VA 22070
703-471-4291

Softronics Computer Services has released the HC-PTRZ System for computer control of appliances and lights. The device allows you to control the popular BSR LTD BSR X-10 control system. The software included provides a screen presentation to allow you to conveniently set up schedules for turning on and off various appliances and lights.
Requires—TRS-80 Level II Model I, 16K Cassette
Softronics Computer Services
P.O.Box 1465
Mesa, AZ 85201

Robots

MINIROVER 5 (MICROBOT) is a tabletop robot arm, remote-controllable by a microcomputer. It is designed to provide hands-on experience with robotics, artificial intelligence, and automation poblems for computer-controlled arms. The MINIROVER 5 is designed to run with a TRS-80 Level II via a ribbon cable attached to the keyboard. The arm has five joints with a resolution of 0.013" and an 8-ounce capacity. Speed of the arm is a function of the weight of the object being moved and ranges from 2" to 12" per second. The hand is of parallel-jaw construction with a maximum 3" opening. The controlling software is called ARMBASIC and uses some assembly language routines. Another version of the robot arm is called MINIROVER 5/8P and may be used with other microcomputers through a parallel port.

MICROROBOT
1259 El Camino Real, Suite 200
Menlo Park, CA 94025
415-326-6997

Terrapin, Inc. has created a low-cost version of the computer-controlled turtles made famous by Sydney Papert's experiments at MIT. The Terrapin Turtle is available assembled or in a kit. It is linked for control signals and power by an umbilical cable to your microcomputer.

TERRAPIN, Inc.
678 Massachusetts Ave.
Cambridge, MA 02139
617-482-1033

Card Reader (Mark sense)

Chatsworth Data has developed a very useful mark sense card reader for use with the TRS-80 Level II Model I, the Apple II, the CBM/PET, and the SORCERER. The device is called the MR-500 mark sense card reader and reads one card at a time individually inserted. Students could actually do programs on the mark sense cards or the cards could be used for responses in a computer-managed instruction system.

Chatsworth Data Corporatrion
20710 Lassen Street
Chatsworth, CA 91311
213-341-9200

High Speed Cassette

The JPC high-speed cassette system for the TRS-80 Model I loads tapes five times faster. *Micro journal* gave the unit a AAA rating and indicated it was quite reliable. It represents a rapid program load system.

JPC Products Co.
12021 Paisano Ct.
Albuquerque, NM 87112
505-294-4623

Mass Storage ("wafer")

Exatron makes a "wafer" recorder for the TRS-80 Model I which allows program and data recording at about 720 characters per second (about 7200 baud). A 50-foot "wafer" can hold 40K. The Exatron system does not require an expansion interface.

Requires—TRS-80 Level II Model I

Exatron Corporation
3555 Ryder Street
Santa Clara, CA
408-737-7111

Large Floppy Disk Systems (8-inch)

The MEGABOX by Micromation may be used with either a TRS-80 Model I or an Exidy Sorcerer to provide a capacity of 512 K on each side of an 8″ dual drive disk system. It also allows the use of an unmodified CP/M disk operating system for the Sorcerer and a modified CP/M for the TRS-80. When used with the TRS-80 Model I, you do not need a Radio Shack expansion interface, as the Megabox has the equivalent built in.

MICROMATION
1620 Montgomery St.
San Francisco, CA 94111
415-398-0289

Sorrento Valley Associates have developed an 8″ floppy disk controller card for the Apple II. They have also provided DOS modifications with the controller. It is (1) Apple DOS comptaible, (2) can read UCSD PASCAL files, and (3) can read files on CP/M disks.

Available for—Apple II and 48K.

Sorrento Valley Associates
11722 Sorrento Valley Rd.
San Diego, CA 92121

Special Expansion Interfaces

LOBO has developed a new expansion interface for the TRS-80 Level II Model I, used in place of the TRS-80 expansion interface. It allows disk storage space totaling 40 MEGABYTES and 32K RAM internally. It has connectors for 5¼″ and 8″ floppy disk drives and separate bidirectional parallel port just for use with the Model 7710T Winchester 10 MBYTE hard disk drive. It also features Centronics printer port, a screen printer port, two bidirectional microprocessor-controlled serial ports, and an internal clock.

Requires—TRS-80 Level II 16K Model I

LOBO Drives International
935 Camino Del Sun
Goleta, CA 93017
805-685-4546
714-641-1436

Hard Disk System (Non-removable)

Corvus provides a two-package hard disk system. One package is the power supply and othe other contains a 10-million byte (character) hard disk system based on the Winchester technology.

Available for—Apple II and 48K; Sorcerer, 48K and S-100 expansion interface; TRS-80 Model I Level II, 48K and expansion interface; and TRS-80 Model II 64K.

CORVUS Systems Inc.
2029 O'Toole Avenue
San Jose, CA 95131
408-246-0461
TELEX - 910-338-0226

Hard Disk Backup System

The CORVUS MIRROR system uses a standard videocassette to back up their 10 megabyte hard disk systems. The videocassette can hold up to 100-million bytes and can back up a 10 megabyte hard disk in 10 minutes. The MIRROR interfaces the videocassette to the hard disk system. It can use the VHS, Beta, or V-matic recorders. It can be used in the CORVUS hard disk systems used with APPLE II; TRS-80 Model I and Model II; and SORCERER.

CORVUS Systems
900 S. Winchester Blvd.
San Jose, CA 95128
408-246-0461

Cartridge Hard Disk Systems (Removable)

Cameo Data Systems markets a hard disk system which has a 5 MBYTE removable cartridge hard disk and a 5 MBYTE fixed hard disk. They provide interfaces to the TRS-80 Model I and Model II, the Apple II, and the Sorcerer through the Sorcerer S-100 expansion interface.

Requires—Please check directly with the manufacturer

CAMEO Data Systems, Inc.
1626 Clementine
Anaheim, CA 92802
714-535-1682

Resource Sharing With Multiple Computers

Corvus provides two very useful products. One is a 10 megabyte (10,000,000 characters) hard disk, based on the Winchester technology. The second is a device called a CONSTELLATION (a multiplexer) which allows eight devices to be hooked up to the hard disk simultaneously. This could allow eight microcomputers to access the same files. By connecting nine CONSTELLATIONs together one could have a 64-microcomputer system accessing the same disk. At least one of the microcomputers should also have floppy disks.

Available for—Apple II and 48K; SORCERER, 48K, and S-100 expansion interface; and TRS-80 Model I Level II, 48K and expansion interface.

CORVUS Systems Inc.
2029 O'Toole Avenue
San Jose, CA 95131
408-246-0461
TWX: 910-338-0226

NEECO has placed on the market a device called MULTI-CLUSTER which allows up to eight CBM/PETS to access one CBM/PET 2040 dual floppy disk system. It allows each terminal to perform random access, sequential access, all OS (disk operating system) commands, and user files.

Available for—CBM/PET.

NEECO
679 Highland Avenue
Needham, MA 02194
617-449-1760
TELEX - 9510201

Radio Shack has developed a device called the Network I Controller for use on the TRS-80 Level II Model I. The Network I Controller allows up to 16 TRS-80 Level II 16K Model I computers to be interfaced to a TRS-80 Level II disk system. The TRS-80 Level II 16K computers can load and save programs from disk (one computer at a time). It is primarily a program load/save device which allows minimal resource sharing.

RADIO SHACK
700 One Tandy Center
Fort Worth, TX 76102

Telephone Coupler (MODEM)

Micro Peripherals has developed a device called the CONNECTION for use with all TRS-80 Model I and II microcomputers. It provides a simple way to interface to a telephone circuit in order to access data bases and time-sharing systems. Basically it comes with a Level II 16K terminal program for half and full duplex. A variety of optional programs include a smart terminal program and a Dow Jones stock management package.

Available for—TRS-80 Model I Level I; TRS-80 Model I Level II; and TRS-80 Model II.

Micro Peripherals Inc.
Box 529
Mercer Island, WA 98040
206-454-3303

Novation has released the CAT, an originate/receive acoustic coupler/modem, for use with computers which have an RS-232-C interface. The device allows your computer to be the host computer (receive) or the terminal (originate). The choice of modes is switch-selectable. You must, of course, have the appropriate software (terminal program) to use the modem. The CAT is currently available directly from some of the microcomputer manufacturers as well as Novation and its dealers.

NOVATION, Inc.
18664 Oxnard Street
Tarzanna, CA 91356
800-423-5410

Radio Shack has released an acoustic coupler called telephone Interface II. This is in fact the CAT modem in silver and black. It has both originate (terminal) and receive (host) modes. It can be used with any RS-232-C interface and computer.

Requires (for Radio Shack)—TRS-80 Level II Model I, expansion interface, 16K, and RS-232-C interface.

Radio Shack
700 One Tandy Center
Fort Worth, TX 76102

CHAPTER 6

Service and Maintenance

The microcomputer, like other equipment, needs service and maintenance. Some natural precautions which can extend the life and usefulness of your microcomputer include:

- Turn off microcomputer and accessories, especially disk drives, if you are not going to use equipment for an extended period of time.
- Provide a cover for your keyboard to keep dust from setting into it.
- Keep cassettes and diskettes in as clean an environment as possible.

Appliance microcomputers are becoming very reliable. In fact, of the several microcomputers in the author's microcomputer teaching laboratory, only the very earliest machines have required service or repair.

In general, problems with appliance microcomputers fall into four main categories:

- problems in reading programs or data from tape
- multiple characters on screen from one key press on keyboard
- mysterious changing values in variables or programs and
- problems in reading programs or data from disk.

The cassette problem usually stems from one of three causes:

- bad head alignment in the cassette recorder
- variations in speed in the cassette recorder
- a problem in the cassette interface circuitry.

Your dealer can usually help with the head alignment; the other two problems usually require detailed service at a qualified repair center.

Multiple copies of the same character on the videoscreen are usually the result of dust in the keyboard. A vacuum cleaner can help clear some problems but sometimes a dealer or service center may have to clean the actual key contacts.

Mysterious changing values or characters in your program listing are the result of memory becoming nonfunctional. Use of a memory test program can help locate the fault; your dealer can then help replace the offending memory chip.

Problems in reading programs from disk is usually due to a speed change. This can occur when:
- the drive which originally recorded the disk runs at a very different speed from the drive being used to read the disk
- the speed of your disk drive changes over time
- the speed of your disk drive changes as the result of changes in the power line voltage.

If you suspect changes in your disk drive speed, your dealer or service center should check and adjust your drive. If you suspect line voltage fluctuation, you need a constant voltage source such as a SOLA power supply.

Some microcomputer manufacturers are now supplying test programs to exercise the complete system and pinpoint any problems; some software companies are also selling programs for this purpose. See the UTILITIES section of the chapter on languages and disk operating systems.

Both Apple and Radio Shack are developing substantial service center programs for quick repair or service when needed. Radio Shack, for example, has over 50 regional service centers. Other computer companies are investigating service carried out at a service center for another company (usually a minicomputer company). Some provide service only at the dealer or factory.

A good dealership should offer loaner equipment or be able to rent you replacement equipment during the repair period.

It should, however, be stressed that the author's experience with a wide variety of appliance microcomputers suggests a very high degree of reliability.

CHAPTER 7

CAI Languages, CMI Systems, Graphics and Futureworld: CAI

Computer-assisted instruction lessons can be programed in almost any computer language. It should be noted, however, that there are over 30 computer-assisted instruction languages; some of these are directly related to each other. Why are there any specialized computer-assisted instruction languages? The answer can be broken into four parts:

- Computer-assisted instruction languages typically have a limited set of commands and are therefore easy to learn to use.
- Computer-assisted instruction languages usually have some special answer-processing functions. The learner's answer may be analyzed for one particular word or phrase. The learner may be allowed to misspell words and still be considered correct.
- Computer-assisted instruction languages usually automatically keep track of student performance and record it on a cassette or diskette. They also make it possible for a teacher to view or list any given student's performance record.
- Virtually all computer-assisted instruction languages are interactive. That is to say, the learner constantly views information and responds to questions at a computer terminal until finished with the lesson.

Computer-based learning systems which do not function interactively through a lesson are usually lumped under the rubric *computer-managed instruction* (CMI). Not all computing languages are interactive.

The major design intent of computer-assisted instruction languages was to provide the previously mentioned abilities and some basic computational capability for use by teachers. It was assumed that teachers should be able to use the CAI languages without being experienced programers. In addition, the primary use projected was tutorial, based upon sets of questions and answers.

If we wish to do computer-assisted instruction on appliance microcomputers, what are our options?

- Use a general purpose language such as BASIC or PASCAL. This would entail writing special purpose subroutines for such

57

things as answer processing and student record keeping.
- Write your own version of a language such as PILOT in the language BASIC. A good beginning reference is "A BASIC PILOT" by Charles Shapiro, *People's Computers* (magazine), Sept.-Oct. 1977, 6(2).
- Purchase a copy of the CAI language PILOT designed to run on your microcomputer. See the RESOURCES section in this chapter for more details.
- Obtain experimental copies of other CAI languages such as MUMPS, LOGO, or SMALLTALK. Dr. Richard Walters of the University of California, Davis, has been developing a version of the MUMPS language for use on the CP/M disk operating system. A good reference on MUMPS is "A Touch of Mumps" by Joan Zimmerman, *Creative Computing* (magazine), November 1979, 5(11). There are rumors that a version of SMALLTALK, the Xerox Dynabook language, may be made available soon for Z-80 based microcomputers.
- Purchase or develop your own course development system. The only one on the market currently is GENIS I from Bell and Howell Microcomputer Systems.

Now, just what would be involved in preparing BASIC subroutines for answer processing and student record keeping? The following section gives some example subroutines that could be used as a part of each CAI program you would write in BASIC.

Basic Subroutines For CAI
Keyword Answering Processing

The first efforts at answer processing involved exact answer match. After initial experimentation, teachers discovered that exact answer matching simply was not effective for many types of tutorial lessons. For example, the student's answer to a question might include the same words in a different order and therefore be counted wrong. The exact answer match implicitly required exact order as well.

This dilemma led to the development of keyword answer processors. In this case, the author specified a keyword and if that word occurred anywhere in the student's response, the response was considered correct. Embellishments quickly became necessary and included such things as (1) multiple keywords and (2) allowing the keyword to be embedded in a larger word. The latter feature allowed the student to respond with the plural form or past tense of the author's answer and still be considered correct.

After further experimentation it was found that exact order of keywords was important and desirable for some lessons. Consequently, the next major embellishment of keyword processors allowed stipulation of exact order or no order. These developments in keyword processors were not only very useful in the standard automated lesson but opened the way for experimentation with simulated conversational interaction. Counselor-patient types of simulations became possible if the teacher could specify anticipated questions or question sequences which might reasonably occur in real life situations.

The developments were useful in computer-assisted instruction applications but basically were available only in CAI languages. The actual implementation of answer processors usually treats the processors as language functions with parameters.

The generalized keyword subroutine presented here was designed to allow specification by the author of up to five keywords and to allow the author to specify how many must be matched in order to be considered correct.

A general procedure for keyword answer processing is outlined as follows:

1. Compare each author keyword with student's response.
2. If a keyword matches, increment the match counter.
3. Compare the match counter with the author's specified number of matches. If equal, print a correct response message, record indication of correct response, and record the student's actual response. Blank the answer variable. Return to calling routine.
4. If no match in step 3, check to see if all keywords have been compared without success. If so, print an incorrect response and record the student's actual response. Blank the answer variable. Return to the calling routine.

General Design of CAI Program Using Keyword Answer Processing

The design of an answer processing routine is dependent to some extent upon the design of the calling program.

Most CAI languages treat lessons as blocks of information to be presented to the student. The block may be composed of (1) information to be displayed, (2) question, (3) specified answers to be compared to a student's response, and (4) actions to be performed dependent upon the quality of the student's response.

Example of 'Block'

A suggested block in BASIC would be as follows:

```
500 PRINT "NAME A PROPERTY OF COLOR"
505 REM --- STUDENT RESPONSE VARIABLE IS A$AS
         IS THE SAME
506 REM --- IN ALL BLOCKS
510 INPUT A$
520 REM --- R IS NUMBER OF BLOCK IN THE PROGRAM;
         K IS THE
521 REM --- NUMBER OF KEYWORDS TO MATCH
530 R=9: K=1
540 REM --- AUTHOR SPECIFIED KEYWORD
550 A$(1)="HUE"
560 A$(2)="VALUE"
570 A$(3)="INTENSITY"
580 REM --- CALL KEYWORD SUBROUTINE
590 GOSUB 7000
```

Design of Keyword Subroutine

The keyword subroutine presented in this article requires the following extended BASIC features:
- STRINGS (length at least equal to 70 characters)
- MID$ (A$,K,J)
- LEN (A$)

The keyword subroutine requires the following unique variables:
- K2 (number of matches)
- K (number of keywords to match—see BLOCK design)
- K1 (actual number of author keywords)
- A$ (string variable which holds student answer)
- R$ (I,J) (string matrix used to record student responses and performance record)
- A(5) (numeric matrix used to hold length of keyword strings)

The keyword routine uses only two temporary variables (I and J). They are used as loop counter variables.

The keyword subroutine allows the following keyword checks:
- Specification of single keyword match from field of 1 to 5 author-specified keywords
- The keyword is treated as a root keyword; consequently, it will allow the occurrence of the keyword with prefix or suffix in the student response.

Now let's take a look at the actual BASIC language subroutines.

KEYWORD ANSWER PROCESSING PROGRAM LISTING

```
1 REM --- CLEAR VARIABLE SPACE AND ASSIGN 1000 BYTES TO STRINGS
2 CLEAR 1000
9 REM --- DECLARE NUMERIC AND STRING MATRICS
10 DIM A(5), A$(5), R$(10,3)
95 REM --- FIRST "BLOCK" OF INSTRUCTIONAL MATERIAL
96 REM      DISPLAY QUESTION AND REQUEST RESPONSE
97 REM         A$ IS USED AS A GENERAL ANSWER VARIABLE FOR ALL
98 REM          "BLOCKS"
100 PRINT:PRINT:PRINT "WHAT IS ONE PROPERTY OF COLOR";: INPUT  A$
105 REM --- THE VARIABLE "R" IS USED TO NUMBER THE BLOCKS AND
106 REM      IS SUBSEQUENTLY USED AS AN INDEX TO THE STUDENT
107 REM      RECORD MATRIX "R$(R,C)"
108 REM      THE VARIABLE "K" IS USED BY THE TEACHER TO SPECIFY
109 REM      THE NUMBER OF KEYWORDS REQUIRED FOR A CORRECT RESPONSE
110 R=1:K=1
115 REM --- THE SUBSCRIPTED STRING VARIABLE A$(N) IS USED BY
116 REM      THE TEACHER TO HOLD THE KEYWORDS CONSIDERED TO BE
117 REM      CORRECT ANSWERS
120 A$(1)="VALUE":A$(2)="HUE":A$(3)="INTENSITY"
125 REM --- CALL KEYWORD PROCESSOR SUBROUTINE (THE SUBROUTINE
126 REM      JUDGES CORRECTNESS OF RESPONSE AND AUTOMATICALLY
127 REM      RECORDS THE INDICATION OF CORRECTNESS IN R$(R,C)
130 GOSUB 7000
195 REM --- ANOTHER INSTRUCTIONAL "BLOCK" BEGINS HERE.  THE
196 REM      STRUCTURE IS THE SAME AS FOR BLOCK 1 (R=1).
200 PRINT:PRINT:PRINT "NAME TWO PROPERTIES OF COLOR:
210 INPUT A$
220 R=2:K=2
230 A$(1)="INTENSITY":A$(2)="VALUE":A$(3)="HUE"
240 GOSUB 7000
295 REM --- "BLOCK 3" BEGINS HERE AND HAS THE SAME STRUCTURE
296 REM      AS THE PRECEEDING BLOCKS.
300 PRINT:PRINT:PRINT "NAME ALL THREE PROPERTIES OF COLOR:
310 INPUT A$
320 R=3:K=3
330 A$(1)="HUE":A$(2)="INTENSITY":A$(3)="VALUE"
340 GOSUB 7000
495 REM --- THE NEXT STATEMENT CONCLUDES THE BLOCKS SUPPLIES
496 REM      TO TEST THE KEYWORD PROCESSOR SUBROUTINE.
500 GOTO 9999
6994 REM
6995 REM --- ****** THE KEYWORD PROCESSOR SUBROUTINE ******
7000 K2=0
7005 REM --- DETERMINE THE LENGTHS OF THE AUTHORS KEYWORDS
7010 A(1)=LEN(A$(1))
7020 A(2)=LEN(A$(2))
7030 A(3)=LEN(A$(3))
7040 A(4)=LEN(A$(4))
7050 A(5)=LEN(A$(5))
7055 REM --- DETERMINE HOW MANY KEYWORDS WERE SUPPLIED FOR
7056 REM      TEST BY THE AUTHOR
7060 FOR I=1 TO 5
7070 IF A(I)=0 THEN 7090
7080 NEXT I
7085 REM --- THE VARIABLE K1 CONTAINS THE ACTUAL NUMBER OF
7086 REM      KEYWORDS IN THE AUTHORS LIST
7090 K1=I
```

```
7095 REM --- COMPARE THE NUMBER OF KEYWORDS SPECIFIED FOR MATCH
7096 REM     WITH THE NUMBER OF KEYWORDS IN THE LIST.  IF
7097 REM     K IS GREATER THAN K1 THEN ASSUME ALL IN THE
7098 REM     LIST MUST MATCH.
7100 IF K>K1 THEN K=K1
7110 I=1
7115 REM --- CHECK TO SEE IF CURRENT KEYWORD BEING TESTED
7116 REM     IS EMPTY (IE, HAS NO CHARACTERS), IF SO TERMINATE
7117 REM     THE TEST SEQUENCE.
7120 IF A(I)=0 THEN 7200
7125 REM --- COMPARE THE CURRENT KEYWORD WITH ALL SEQUENCES OF
7126 REM     CHARACTERS IN THE STUDENT'S ANSWER.
7130 FOR J=1 TO LEN (A$)
7140 IF MID$(A$,J,A(I))<>A$(I) THEN 7150
7141 REM --- IF MATCH,. INCREMENT MATCH COUNTER
7142 K2=K2+1
7144 GOTO 7160
7150 NEXT J
7155 REM --- COMPARE MATCH COUNTER WITH THE NUMBER OF KEYWORDS
7156 REM     SPECIFIED AS NECESSARY FOR CORRECT RESPONSE.  IF
7166 REM     NEGATIVE MESSAGE TO THE STUDENT.
7157 REM     EQUAL, PRINT POSITIVE MESSAGE FOR STUDENT.  IF NOT,
7158 REM     CHECK TO SEE IF ALL KEYWORDS IN LIST HAVE BEEN
7159 REM     HAVE BEEN TESTED.
7160 IF K2=K THEN PRINT "RIGHT":GOTO 7230
7165 REM --- IF ALL KEYWORDS IN THE LIST HAVE BEEN TESTED, PRINT
7170 IF I=5  THEN 7200
7180 I=I+1
7190 GOTO 7120
7200 PRINT "WRONG!"
7205 REM --- STORE INDICATION OF WRONG RESPONSE IN THE STUDENT RECORD
7206 REM     MATRIX
7210 R$(R,3)="-"
7220 GOTO 7240
7225 REM --- STORE INDICATION OF CORRECT RESPONSE IN THE STUDENT
7226 REM     MATRIX
7230 R$(R,3)="+"
7235 REM --- STORE ACTUAL STUDENT RESPONSE IN THE STUDENT RECORD
7236 REM     MATRIX
7240 R$(R,2)=A$
7245 REM --- BLANK RESPONSE VARIABLE.
7250 A$=""
7255 REM --- RETURN TO THE CALLING "BLOCK".
7260 RETURN
9999 END
```

Answer processing using keywords represents a very powerful tool in the development of conversational simulations. Programs can be devised to carry on a useful conversation in a limited context.

While keyword answer processing opened new horizons in the development of tutorial lessons, teachers encountered problems with students who could not spell or type accurately. These problems suggested the need for an answer processor to phonetically encode responses and thus avoid problems with typographic and spelling errors.

A very basic but interesting phonetic answer processor algorithm was developed through a project funded by the National Science Foundation. The project resulted in the development of a CAI language called PLANIT that was to be "machine-independent." It successfully met that goal, with the only restrictions being a 24-bit word size (minimum) and access to a FORTRAN IV compiler. The phonetic algorithm used in PLANIT is quoted verbatim in this article.

Basic Phonetic Processor Procedure

The general procedure for a phonetic answer processor in BASIC is as follows:
1. Disassemble the answer or response string into single character strings.
2. Sequentially convert each single character string into its phonetic equivalent using the PLANIT PHONETIC ALGORITHM (procedure).
3. Reassemble phonetic characters equivalents into a single string.
4. Return to calling program for comparison of phonetic equivalent response to a phonetic equivalent answer specified by the lesson author.

*Phonetic Encoding and Formulas Processing**

The phonetic answer processor subroutine requires the following extended BASIC features:
- STRINGS (length at least equal to 70 characters)
- MID$(A$,J,1)
- LEN(A$)

Phonetic Encoding

The phonetic encoding process is accomplished in four steps:
1. Letter Equivalent: All letters are transformed into their let-

---

*Bennick, F.D., & Frye, C. H., PLANIT Language Reference Manual. System Development Corporation TM-(L)-4422/002/01, Oct. 1970. (APPENDIX E)

ter equivalents. Any remaining characters including blanks are unchanged. The letter in Row 1 is transformed into the letter immediately below in Row 2. PLANIT ignores all other characters.

Row 1 ABCDEFGHIJKLMNOPQRSTUVWXYZ (original letter)

Row 2 ABCDABCHACCLMMABCRCDABHCAC (letter equivalent)

2. The H Replacement: Each H in a word is transformed to the preceding letter provided the character is a letter. If not a letter (e.g., a blank), H is unchanged.

3. Elimination of Successive Identical Consonants: All but the first element of an uninterrupted sequence of a single consonant are eliminated, (e.g., CC = C, TT = T).

4. Elimination of A's: All vowels, transformed A's, are eliminated unless A is the first character of the word to be encoded. The final word contains only consonants and a leading A if there is one.

Examples:

Original Word	Steps			
	1	2	3	4
PHONETIC	BHAMADAC	BBAMADAC	BAMADAC	BMDC
HAZARD	HACARD	HACARD	HACARD	HCRD
ON-LINE	AM-LAMA	AM-LAMA	AM-LAMA	AM-LM
AWHILE	AHHALA	AAAALA	AAAALA	AL

The phonetic subroutine requires the following unique variables:

• B$ (phonetic encoded answer)
• A$ (string variable to hold student response)
• R$(I,J) (string matrix used to hold individual characters from student response or author answer)
• B$(73) (string matrix used to hold individual characters from student response or author answer)

The phonetic subroutine uses only two temporary variables (J and K). They are used as loop counter variables and index pointers for matrices.

The phonetic answer processor subroutine is designed to be called to process both the author's answer and the student's response (on separate GOSUB calls). The phonetic response processor can handle character strings up to 70 characters in length with embedded blanks and punctuation. The only restriction is that the use of a comma in the student's answer may produce a syntax error depending on the BASIC interpreter being used.

The listing of a sample minilesson (one "block") and the phonetic subroutine follow.

Phonetic Response Answer Processor Program Listing

```
1 REM --- CLEAR VARIABLE SPACE AND ASSIGN 500 BYTES TO STRINGS
2 CLEAR 500
9 REM --- DECLARE STRING MATRICES FOR PHONETIC SUBROUTINE
10 DIM B$(73)
15 REM --- DECLARE STRING MATRIX FOR STUDENT PERFORMANCE RECORDS
16 REM     THE R DIMENSION REFERS TO THE NUMBER OF "BLOCKS"
17 REM     ENCOUNTERED BY THE STUDENT.  THE C DIMENSION REFERS
18 REM     TO (1) BLOCK NUMBER, (2) ACTUAL RESPONSE, AND (3)
19 REM     THE RESULT OF COMPARING RESPONSE WITH ANSWER
20 DIM R$(30,3)
70 B$(0)=" "
80 I=0
95 REM --- FIRST "BLOCK" OF INSTRUCTIONAL MATERIALS.
96 REM         PRESENT QUESTION - - -
100 PRINT  "WHO WAS THE FIRST PRESIDENT OF THE U.S."
105 REM --- THE VARIABLE R REFERS TO THE BLOCK NUMBER.
106 REM     THE VARIABLE I IS USED TO INDICATE THE NUMBER OF
107 REM     ATTEMPTS IN THE LESSON.  THE MATRIX R$(R,C)
108 REM     IS USED TO HOLD A RECORD OF THE STUDENT'S
109 REM     PERFORMANCE BLOCK BY BLOCK.
110 R=1:I=I+1:R$(I,1)=STR$(R)
115 REM --- A$ IS USED TO HOLD THE AUTHOR SPECIFIED ANSWER
120 A$="WASHINGTON"
125 REM --- GOTO PHONETIC SUBROUTINE AND CONVERT ANSWER TO
126 REM     PHONETIC REPRESENTATION.  RETURN IT IN B$.
130 GOSUB 8000
135 REM --- MOVE PHONETIC REPRESENTATION FROM TEMPORARY VARIABLE
136 REM     B$ TO P$.
140 P$=B$
145 REM --- MOVE STUDENT RESPONSE TO THE QUESTION.
146 REM     A$ IS AGAIN USED TO HOLD DATA TO BE PASSED TO
147 REM     PHONETIC SUBROUTINE.
150 INPUT A$
155 REM --- STORE STUDENT'S ACTUAL RESPONSE IN RECORD MATRIX
160 R$(I,2)=A$
165 REM --- GOTO PHONETIC SUBROUTINE AND CONVERT RESPONSE TO
166 REM     REPRESENTATION.  RETURN IT IN B$.
170 GOSUB 8000
175 REM --- COMPARE B$ WITH P$.
180 IF P$<>B$ THEN 210
185 REM --- RECORD CORRECT RESPONSE INDICATOR
190 R$(I,3)="+"
195 REM --- PRINT FEEDBACK MESSAGE TO STUDENT
200 PRINT "RIGHT!":GOTO 230
205 REM --- RECORD INCORRECT RESPONSE INDICATOR
210 R$(I,3)="-"
```

```
215 REM --- PRINT FEEDBACK MESSAGE TO STUDENT
220 PRINT "WRONG!"
225 REM --- PROCEED TO NEXT FRAME
229 REM *** END OF TEST OF PHONETIC SUBROUTINE
230 GOTO 9999
7996 REM ******** PHONETIC SUBROUTINE ********
7998 REM --- SET UP VARIABLES FOR COUNTERS
8000 K=1:J=1
8002 B$=" "
8005 REM --- PLACE EACH LETTER/CHAR IN ANSWER INTO SEPARATE CELL
8010 IF J>LEN (A$) THEN 8200
8020 B$(K)=MID$(A$,J,1)
8022 REM --- TRANSFORM ANSWER LETTERS INTO LETTER EQUIVALENTS. BLANKS
8024 REM      REMAIN UNCHANGED. LETTERS TRANSFORMED AS FOLLOWS:
8026 REM
8028 REM  ORIG. A B C D E F G H I J K L M N O P Q R S T U V W X Y Z
8029 REM EQUIV. A B C D A B C H A C C L M M A B C R C D A B H C A A
8030 IF (B$(K)="E" OR B$(K)="I" OR B$(K) ="O" THEN B$(K) ="A"
8040 IF B$ (K) = "U" OR B$(K) = "Y" THEN B$(K) = "A"
8050 IF B$(K)="F" OR B$(K)="P" OR B$(K) ="V" THEN B$(K)="B"
8060 IF B$(K)="G" OR B$(K)="J" OR B$(K)="K" THEN B$(K)="C"
8070 IF B$(K)="Q" OR B$(K)="S" THEN B$(K)="C"
8080 IF B$(K)="X" OR B$(K)="Z" THEN B$(K)="C"
8090 IF B$(K)="W" THEN B$(K)="H"
8100 IF B$(K)="N" THEN B$(K)="M"
8110 IF B$(K)="T" THEN B$(K)="D"
8115 REM --- TRANSFORM H INTO PREVIOUS LETTER UNLESS IT BEGINS WORD
8120 IF B$(K)="H" AND B$(K-1)<>" " THEN B$(K)=B$(K-1)
8130 IF B$(K)="A" THEN 8150
8135 REM --- REPEATED CONSONANT DELETED
8140 IF B$(K)=B$(K-1) THEN B$(K)=" ":K=K-1
8145 REM --- REPEATED A DELETED
8150 IF B$(K)="A" AND B$(K-1)="A" THEN B$(K)=" ":K=K-1
8155 REM --- DELETE A AFTER CONSNANTS
8160 IF B$(K)="A" AND B$(K-1)<>" " THEN B$(K)=" ":K=K-1
8165 REM --- A AFTER A BLANK ALLOWED (EG AT START OF A WORD)
8170 J=J+1
8180 K=K+1
8190 GOTO 8010
8200 FOR M=1 TO LEN(A$)
8220 B$=B$+B$(M)
8230 NEXT M
8240 RETURN
9999 PRINT:PRINT "******* END OF PHONETIC SUBROUTINE TEST********":END
```

A General Purpose Student Record Subroutine

There are three major purposes for maintaining records of student performance: (1) The learning process is enhanced when performance quality is revealed to the learner immediately, in the context of the total task or lesson; (2) records indicating student performance on specific items allow the teacher to provide more effective guidance; and (3) records can be used to assess the effectiveness of the learning materials and to identify areas of the task needing redesign.

The first purpose described above can be accomplished by the use of simple correct and incorrect answer counters in the form:

line #R=R+l (Right Answer)

or

line 3w=W+ 1 (Wrong Answer)

The appropriate counter is incremented after judging the student's response. At the end of the program, the lesson author would probably use something similar to the following code:

Line #   PRINT "YOU GOT"; R; "RIGHT WITH"; W; "WRONG!"

Line #   PRINT "YOUR OVERALL PERFORMANCE WAS"; INT(R/R W)*100);% CORRECT."

The procedure just described is entirely student-oriented; i.e. no records are kept for teacher use. The second and third purposes for maintaining performance records are to make information available for teachers.

Design Layout of Student Records

The design of a more pervasive student records procedure may be summarized as follows:

1. Identify the information to be retained.
2. Specify matrix layout required to maintain the information.
3. Identify items to be manipulated or defined for each question/answer block presented.
4. Specify information to be presented in a summary report form.
5. Specify completed record report form.

The design presented here is predicated on a machine with no disk or machine with a BASIC that permits storage of array/matrix data.

1. *Information to be retained.* It is possible for a learner to encounter the same question/answer item more than once. Therefore, it is useful to know the actual sequence encountered by the student. Also, it is occasionally useful to see the student's actual response to an item, and to identify which block of information was encountered. Last but by no means least, one needs the result of the response judgment.

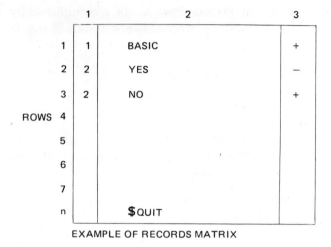

EXAMPLE OF RECORDS MATRIX

Figure 14. Examples of Records Matrix

2. *Matrix layout.* It is probably most convenient to use a two-dimensional string matrix for storage of the performance record. The author has arbitrarily designated the matrix as R$(R,C).

3. *Items to be defined or manipulated in a block.* Most CAI languages treat lessons as discrete "chunks" of information. The "chunks" may be information to be printed, questions and answers, or a combination. We will refer to such an arrangement as a *block*. The structure of a block would appear as follows:

```
Line #R=n (Defines number of block)
Line #I=I+1 (The Ith time the student has encountered
      an item; used as a row index to records matrix)
Line #R$(I,1)-STR$(R) (Stores a string representation
      of the block number in the record matrix)
Line #PRINT "WHAT IS THE MOST AVAILABLE MICROCOMPUTER
      LANGUAGE"
Line #INPUT A$
Line #R$(I,2)=A$ (Store student answer in matrix)
Line #A$(1)="BASIC"
Line #A$(2)="EXTENDED BASIC"
Line #IF A$ A$(1) AND A$ A$(2)THEN LINE #n
Line #R$(I,3)="+":PRINT "RIGHT!"
Line #GOTO LINE #n+1
Line #n R$(I,3)="-":PRINT "WRONG!"
Line #n+1 GOTO NEXT BLOCK
Note:  After last block, Set I=I=1 THEN R$(I,2)="$QUIT"
(This signals the end of the entries in the matrix)
```

4. *Summary report.* The summary report should print a report heading and the columnar headings "block number" and "judgment". It should also print the total number correct, total number incorrect, and a performance percentage.

5. *Complete report.* The complete report should include a column for the actual response as well as all the data for the summary report.

The subroutines are actually only the routines used to print the contents of the records. The records are actually generated through the blocks. The subroutines are executed after the student completes the lesson by typing GOTO n where n is the starting line number for the desired report.

The following listing shows the subroutines and two example blocks.

```
10 CLEAR 500
50 DIM A$(5)
60 DIM R$(100,3)
80 PRINT:PRINT:PRINT "  CAI LESSON AND DEMONSTRATION OF STUDENT RECO
RDS
"
90 PRINT:PRINT
100 INPUT "WHAT IS YOUR NAME";N$
110 I=0
115 REM ******** FIRST BLOCK IN LESSON ********
120 R=1:I=I+1:R$(I,1)+STR$(R)
130 PRINT "NAME THE MOST POPULAR LANGUAGE ON MICRO-COMPUTERS CURRENTLY"
140 INPUT A$
150 A$(1)="BASIC"
160 A$(2)="EXTENDED BASIC"
170 A$(3)="MITS BASIC"
180 A$(4)="8K BASIC"
190 R$(I,2)=A$
200 IF A$<>A$(1) AND A$<>A$(2) AND A$<>A$(3) AND A$<>A$(4) THEN 250
210 R$(I,3)="+"
220 GOTO 270
250 R$(I,3)="-"
260 REM ******** SECOND BLOCK IN LESSON ********
265 REM --- NOTE THAT THIS BLOCK REQUIRES THE STUDENT TO GET THE ANSWER
266 REM     CORRECT BEFORE HE CAN MOVE AHEAD IN THE LESSON.
270 R=2:I=I+1:R$(I,1)=STR$(R)
280 PRINT "IS IT AVAILABLE IN ALL MICRO COMPUTERS"
290 INPUT A$
300 A$(1)="NO"
310 R$(I,2)=A$
320 IF A$=A$(1) THEN R$(I,3)="+":GOTO 350
330 PRINT "TRY AGAIN!"
340 R$(I,3)="-":GOTO 270
350 GOTO 9995
9000 REM --- STUDENT RECORD PRINT SUBROUTINES
9002 REM     (1) SUMMARY FORM (INCLUDES BLOCK NUMBER AND RESPONSE
9003 REM         INDICATOR)
9004 REM     (2) COMPLETE STUDENT RECORD (BLOCK NUMBER, ACTUAL
9005 REM         STUDENT RESPONSE, AND RESPONSE INDICATOR)
```

```
9010 PRINT:PRINT:PRINT "****** STUDENT PERFORMANCE RECORD FOR ";N$';" ***
***"
9020 PRINT TAB(18);"(SUMMARY FORM)"
9030 PRINT
9040 PRINT "BLOCK NUMBER";TAB(15):"ANSWER JUDGEMENT"
9045 REM --- R IS THE VARIABLE USED TO TALLY THE CORRECT RESPONSES.
9046 REM     W IS THE VARIABLE USED TO TALLY THE INCORRECT RESPONSES.
9047 REM     N IS THE VARIABLE USED TO COUNT THE TOTAL RESPONSES.
9050 PRINT:R=0:W=0:N=0
9055 REM --- MAIN LOOP USED TO EXAMINE STUDENT PERFORMANCE ITEM BY ITEM
9056 REM     INFORMATION EACH ITEM IS PRINTED ON A LINE.
9057 REM     WHEN "$QUIT" IS FOUND IN THE ACTUAL ANSWER AREA FOR THE
9058 REM     LAST ENTRY IN THE RECORDS MATRIX, THE PROGRAM THEN
9059 REM     PRINTS TOTALS AND PERCENTAGE OF PERFORMANCE.
9060 FOR I=1 TO 100
9070 IF R$(I,2)="$QUIT" THEN 9120
9075 REM --- PRINT ITEM (BLOCK) NUMBER AND RESPONSE INDICATOR.
9080 PRINT TAB (5);R$(I,1);TAB(20);R$(I,3)
9085 REM --- COUNT CORRECT RESPONSE
9090 IF R$(I,3)="+" THEN R=R+1
9095 REM --- COUNT INCORRECT RESPONSE
9100 IF R$(I,3)="-" THEN W=W+1
9110 NEXT I
9115 REM --- SET N COUNTER TO ONE LESS THAN I BECAUSE LAST ITEM IN
9116 REM     STUDENT RECORD IS USED FOR FLAG FOR END OF RECORD.
9120 N=I-1
9130 PRINT
9140 PRINT "TOTAL ANSWER BLOCKS SEEN: ";N
9150 PRINT "TOTAL INCORRECT ANSWERS:  ";W
9160 PRINT "TOTAL CORRECT ANSWERS:    ";R
9170 PRINT "    PERFORMANCE PERCENTAGE:  "; INT(R/N*100);"%" ***
****"
9180 PRINT
9190 PRINT "--------------------------------------------------------"
9200 PRINT:PRINT:STOP
9300 PRINT:PRINT:PRINT "****** STUDENT PERFORMANCE RECORD FOR ";N$;" ***
****"
9310 PRINT TAB (18);"(COMPLETE RECORD)"
9320 PRINT
9325 REM --- PRINT BLOCK NUMBER, ACTUAL RESPONSE AND ANSWER JUDGEMENT F
9326 REM     EACH ITEM
9330 PRINT "BLOCK NUMBER";TAB(15);"ACTUAL RESPONSE";TAB(50);"JUDGEMENT"
9340 PRINT:R=0:W=0:N=0
9350 FOR I=1 TO 100
9360 IF R$(I,2)="$QUIT" THEN 9410
9370 PRINT TAB (5);R$(I,1);TAB(15);R$(I,2);TAB(55);R$(I,3)
9380 IF R$(I,3)="+" THEN R=R+1
9390 IF R$(I,3)="-" THEN W=W+1
9400 NEXT I
9410 N=I-1
9420 PRINT
9430 PRINT "TOTAL ANSWER BLOCKS SEEN:  ";N
9440 PRINT "TOTAL INCORRECT ANSWERS:   ";W
9450 PRINT "TOTAL CORRECT ANSWERS:     ";R
9460 PRINT "    PERFORMANCE PERCENTAGE:   ";INT(R/N*100);"%"
9470 PRINT
9480 PRINT "-------------------------------------------------"
9490 PRINT:PRINT:STOP
9995 I=I+1
9996 R$(I,2)="$QUIT"
9999 END
```

Note: This represents the combination of two articles published in the proceedings of the First West Coast Computer Fair; the material also appeared as an article titled "Computer-Assisted Instruction in BASIC" by Franz J. Frederick, *Peoples Computer* (magazine), July-August 1977, 6(1), 51-58.

As you can see, developing keyword and phonetic answer processing subroutines and student record keeping subroutines in BASIC involves a good deal of work. Remember that most good CAI languages and implementations offer at least keyword processing and perhaps automatic record keeping. Only a few provide phonetic response processing. In other words, in a CAI language the things implied in the subroutines just presented are "automatic" and built into the language.

Just what CAI languages or systems are available for the appliance microcomputers?

Resources: CAI Language

APPILOT
(PILOT Language—
interpreter based
on COMMON PILOT
standards)
An easy-to-use computer-
assisted language (CAI).
Allows one to easily create
tutorial learning programs
for APPLE II.
Available for: APPLE II, 32K, with Disk (Integer)

Computer Services
30 Highway 321,N.W.
Hickory, NC 28601
704-294-1616

APPLE PILOT
(PILOT language—Inter-
preter based on Common
PILOT standards)
3rd QTR 1980
Available for: APPLE II, 48K, and Disk II

Apple Computer, Inc.
10260 Bandley Drive
Cupertino, CA 95014
408-996-1010

ARISTOTLE APPLE
(a tutorial program for CAI
activities)

Stoneware Microcomputer
Products
1930 Fourth Street
San Rafael, CA 94901

Available for: APPLE II, 48K, and Disk II

COMMON PILOT
(interpreter)

Lords, Corp.
Specialty Software
P.O.Box 99
Port Angeles, WA 93262
206-457-3064

Available for: TRS-80 Level II, Model I,
expansion interface, 32K,
disk and DOS 2.1 (or better)

CLASSROOM COMPUTER
PACKAGE (computer-
assisted instruction system)

Micro-Educational
P.O.Box 280
Nelson Bay 2315
N.S.W. Australia

Provides a two-disk CAI
authoring and administrative
system. Allows high resolution
graphics, Q/A, tutorials, captions, and text presentation.
Available for: APPLE II, 32K-48K, Disk II

COMPU-MATH
(educational software)

EDU-WARE SERVICE, INC.
Suite 223
22035 Burbank Blvd.

Two-disk package with pretest
for skill determination. Contains six learning
modules to teach use of fractions.
Randomly generates posttests to
determine effectiveness of skill
acquisition. Uses screen
graphics.

Woodland Hills, CA 91367
213-346-6783

Available for: APPLE II, 48K, and Disk II

GENIS I
(CAI System)
Contains the following
programs:

Bell & Howell Microcomputer
Systems
Audio-Visual Products
7100 N. McCormick Rd.
Chicago, IL 60645

1. Course Development
(CSI) allows teacher to automatically create a linear

sequence tutorial learning
program. It is based on a presentation and test model. It
allows a variety of answer
modes.

2. MARK-PILOT—based upon
common PILOT with added
student record keeping features and graphics commands.
Allows branching program
tutorial sequence. Requires
teacher to learn the PILOT
programing commands.

3. SYNER-GENIS—allows
the CDS to call MARK-PILOT
programs for graphics, simulations, and other MARK-
PILOT tutorial lessons.
Available for: APPLE II, 48K, 2 Disk Drives

PET PILOT
(CAI language-interpreter)

Provides full PILOT for PET
with full BASIC calculations
in the c: statements.

D. Gomberg & M. Kemp
7 Gateview Court
San Francisco, CA 94116

Available for: CMB/PET 8K; requires second cassette drive to
generate lessons

PILOT
(CAI language-interpreter)
Provides 10 commands plus
cursor and graphics control
commands.

Dr. Daley
425 Grove Avenue
Berrien Springs, MI 49103
616-471-5514

Available for: CBM/PET 8K with cassettes

PET PILOT
(CAI language
interpreter)
Provides full PILOT with
BASIC

Computer Project
Peninsula School
Peninsula Way
Menlo Park, CA 94025

Available for: CBM/PET 8K with cassette

PILOT INTERPRETERS
(for Z-80 and 8080 based
systems; patched for CP/M
system)
Note: Volume 12 contains
PILOT interpreters and their
source code for changing and
reassembly. You should
acquire this only if you feel
competent in assembly language work. The PILOTs on
this disk are usable on unmodified CP/M systems. Addi-
tional Note: Volume 28 contains some games, a data base
system, and an AGOL-like
language (compiler).

CP/M User's Group
164 West 33rd Street
New York, NY 10024

Available for: Unmodified CP/M systems on 8" floppy disk.

Courseware Development Systems (CMI)

To date only one courseware development system has been mar-
keted as such. Bell and Howell Microcomputer Systems offers the
GENIS I system, which includes:
• the CDS I (the courseware development system)
• the MARK-PILOT system
• SYNER-GENIS, a program that allows a user to combine the
features of CDS I and MARK-PILOT.

CDS I (the courseware development system)

CDS I is used essentially as a management system. It helps a
teacher who is not a programer to create tutorial lessons. It can be
used to create quizzes, and, with MARK-PILOT, for simulations
and graphics. Tutorials and quizzes created in CDS I are sequential in nature; i.e., each section or question must be taken in
sequential order.

CDS I allows:
• presentation of text pages
• question
• specification of correct answers
• specification of wrong answers

- specification of unexpected answers
- specification of a failure message
- hints
- specification of the number of tries before getting the failure message.

In the answer specifications CDS I allows the teacher to:

- enter or control misspellings
- use synonyms
- provide or allow for similar ways of phrasing an answer.

CDS I allows the teacher to request that student records be kept, to specify student enrollment lists, and to modify the enrollment list. CDS I provides the ability to display student performance for the class on either the video display or a printer.

MARK-PILOT

The MARK-PILOT system contains both an authoring segment and a student presentation segment.

The authoring segments allows you to:

- create a PILOT lesson
- modify or edit a PILOT lesson
- keep track of lessons you have already developed
- enroll students for lessons
- obtain grade/statistics report
- modify the student enrollment list
- delete a lesson from the disk.

The student presentation mode:

- allows a student to take a lesson
- keeps student records based on performance in the lesson.

MARK-PILOT has the normal PILOT commands but also allows the author to create low-resolution graphics (based on 40 X 40 dots on the screen). It also allows choice of colors from the PILOT lesson. MARK-PILOT also permits, in the calculation mode, all the calculation features of the BASIC language.

SYNER-GENIS

SYNER-GENIS provides an interesting ability for CDS I and MARK-PILOT to interact with each other. With the use of SYNER-GENIS a learner can be using a lesson in CDS I and CDS I can automatically place the student in a MARK-PILOT lesson. When finished with the MARK-PILOT material, the student is returned immediately to the original location in the CDS I lesson.

CDS I does not have a graphics mode but MARK-PILOT DOES; SYNER-GENIS allows the two to work together to produce graphics for use with a CDS I presentation. Similarly, CDS I does not have branching capability or computational capability but MARK-PILOT does.

The teacher documentation for GENIS I is of generally high quality. Watch for other systems to appear in the marketplace soon.

Information Systems

The only information retrieval systems currently offered for microcomputers are the ones called data base systems. There is quite a range of types of data base systems but almost all make use of disk systems. See Chapter 9 for specific systems.

Watch for the development and marketing of content-and task-specific information retrieval systems in the near future.

Computer Graphics

All current appliance microcomputers offer the ability to create graphics ("drawings") and animations on the video screen. The resolution ranges from 40 X 40 dots to 192 X 256 dots. Some offer 4 to 16 colors. The ability to create graphics and/or new type faces ranges from easy to fairly difficult. Fortunately various software developers have created programs that make it relatively easy to accomplish these tasks.

RESOURCES

Programs to Create Graphics and Type Faces

APPLE PLOT   Apple Computer Inc.
(graphics plotter package)
Creates detailed charts and
graphs.
Available for: APPLE II, 48K, DISK II, Apple Silent Printer or
Qume Sprint 5, appropriate printer controller card

The Designer System   Apple Jack
(high resolution graphics)   12 Monterey Drive
generation   Cherry Valley, MA 01611

Allows creation of high resolution graphics by use of game
paddles or joysticks.
Available for: APPLE II, APPLESOFT ROM, 48K, and DISK II

GRAPHICS MASTER   Micro Data Systems
(graphics generation   Dept. B
program)   7275 Meath Way
         No. Highlands, CA 95660
         916-448-7048
Available for: TRS-80 Level II Model I, 16K, cassette

HIGHER GRAPHICS II   Synergistic Software
(high resolution graphics   5221 120th Ave, SE
generation)   Bellevue, WA 98006
Allows creation of graphics and
animation. Provides four shape
tables with over 100 shapes.
Available for: APPLE II, 32K and DISK II

HIGHER TEXT   Synergistic Software
(high resolution character generation program)
 Available for: APPLE II and DISK II

Master Graphics Reference   SUMWARE
(shows TRS-80 keyboard and   Suite 406
graphics characters in all   537 S. Sequoia Dr.
horizontal and vertical   West Palm Beach, FL 33401
combinations)
Available for: TRS-80 Model I

PICTYPE   Discovery Bay Software Co.
(graphics generation program)   P.O.Box 464
         Port Townsend, WA 98368
Available for: TRS-80 Level II Model I, expansion interface, 32K,
disk

PLOTTER   HSC Computer Services
(graph generator)   P.O.Box 43
         Brooklyn, N.Y. 11236
         212-780-0022

Available for: unmodified CPM (8″) and requires CBASIC 2

Programmable Graphic   North American Software
Sketch Pad (graphics   P.O.Box 1173, Stn. 'B'
generator program)   Downsview, Ontario,
                                    CAN. M3H5V6
Available for: Exidy SORCERER, 16K, cassette

FUTUREWORLD: CAI

The Learning Research Group and Alan Kay of Xerox have developed an interesting personal computer concept called DYNABOOK. The group is proposing that eventually a new personal computer can be developed that would:

- have a complete package size about the size and shape of an ordinary notebook
- have storage capacity for thousands of pages of information, such as letters, poems, simulations, and pictorial images
- have no perceptible response time delay
- be designed so that any owner could "mold and channel its power to his own needs"
- have a medium of communication (language) as simple and powerful as possible (e.g., more powerful than LOGO) and suitable for serious systems design
- be as context-free as possible
- allow real time video synthesis
- allow real time music synthesis.

A very important part of the DYNABOOK concept is the language called SMALLTALK. It is a different language in that major entities are called classes. Each class has specific capabilities; e.g., adding numbers, making sounds, or drawing pictures. Each class contains a series of objects. The art of programing in SMALLTALK centers around the process of routing messages between or among objects in the system. Here are some SMALLTALK examples:

Example   **Explanation**
1. * TURTLE.!   Create a new object * as a "TURTLE"

2. * GO 20!   Draw a line from * initial location "forward" 20 units

3. DO 4 (*GO 30 TURN 90.)!   Draw a square 30 units on a side

In essence, SMALLTALK allows:
- super graphics
- powerful, compact programs
- the ability to create new classes
- multiple independent processes.

At the 1980 NCC show, a group of Texas programers called ROSETTA demonstrated an AD HOC version of SMALLTALK for use on Z-80 microcomputers. The demonstration machine was in fact a Sorcerer. The demonstration was effective and interesting.

Let's let our minds run wild for a moment. An interesting combination of new products and experimental materials could yield an experimental "DYNABOOK" which would have:
- an Apple II microcomputer with 48K, color high resolution graphics, game paddles, and a light pen
- music synthesizer boards, amplifiers, and speakers
- a Microsoft Z-80 card and CP/M disk operating system
- a Z-80 SMALLTALK language
- a videodisc interfaced to the Apple and the SMALLTALK language
- if large scale storage is necessary, a 10 million-character hard disk drive.

It would appear that such a configuration could be a state of the art "DYNABOOK." Because a random access videodisc costs around $5,000 and a 10 million-character disk costs around $5,500 such an experimenters' dream would be expensive now. However, there are rumors of a 4¼" floppy disk capable of storing 5 million characters and hope springs eternal that random access videodiscs will come down to about $1,000.

CHAPTER 8

Time Sharing and Resource Sharing on Microcomputers

In big computing circles and prior to the current crop of very effective microcomputers, time-sharing became popular because the costs of large scale computing, mass storage, and printing could be distributed over a number of users. Computer terminals, however, tended to cost between $1500 and several thousand dollars. Now you can buy very capable microcomputers with extensive memory and some program storage capability and thus avoid time-shared systems.

Once you consider adding disk drives and printers, the cost escalates. This is particularly true if you have, for example, seven microcomputers and want disk file capabilities for each and printing capability. At this point, we have come full circle and now find it desirable to at least resource-share, if not time-share. In this chapter we will consider four systems based on the concept of resource-sharing among a group of microcomputers and one real time-sharing microcomputer system. The latter system is definitely not an appliance microcomputer system.

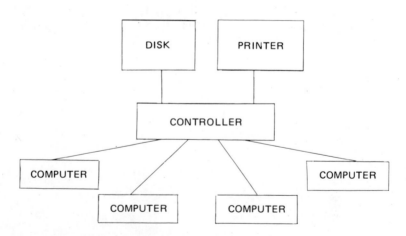

Figure 15. General Network Diagram

In this chapter resource-sharing systems are defined as systems in which each user has a microcomputer connected in a network to share the common resources such as disk storage and printers. The major purpose of the controller in the diagram is to schedule the use of resources by the computers. Because only one computer at a time can actually use the disk drive, the controller must regulate requests to use the resources.

Radio Shack Network I Controller

This resource controller is the least expensive and also the most restricted in function. It allows up to 16 TRS-80s to share the disk drive of a TRS-80 disk system.

The Network I controller allows:

- Simultaneous loading of the same program from the disk system into any or all of the TRS-80s in the network
- Loading of given TRS-80 with a program from disk
- Saving a program to disk by any given TRS-80; the procedure requires an operator at the central disk system and an operator at the student computer station.

The Network I controller doesn't have the ability to control the various requests for system resources; i.e., disk and printer usage. That sort of activity must be monitored and controlled by humans. The network would look like this:

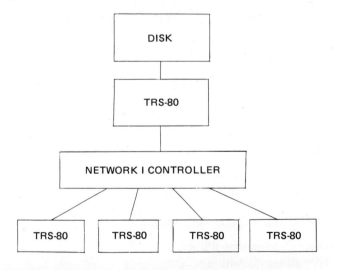

Figure 16. Radio Shack Network I Controller Diagram

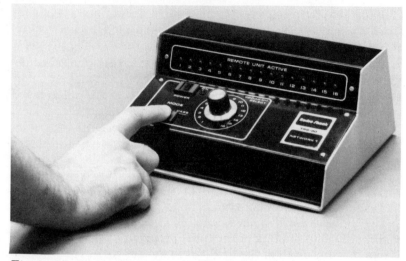

Figure 17. Radio Shack Network I Controller

Nestar Cluster/One

The Nestar Cluster/One Model A allows placing up to 64 Apple IIs in a common resource-sharing network. The network uses one Apple II as a monitor station for the system. The network would look like the following diagram:

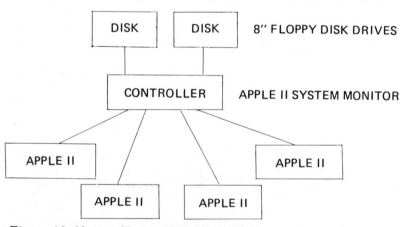

Figure 18. Nestar Cluster/One Model A Diagram

The Nestar Cluster/One allows:

• intercomputer communication
• sharing data

- accessing the same disk files
- no computer in the network to impair the operation of another
- each Apple II to load and save programs
- each Apple II to create and use data files on disk.

Nestar also has Cluster/One models which allow mixing various models of microcomputers for program load and save only. For more information contact:

NESTAR SYSTEMS INC.
430 Sherman Avenue
Palo Alto, CA 94306
415-327-0125
415-494-6267

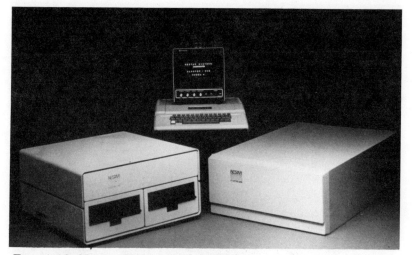

Figure 19. Nestar Cluster/One System

Corvus Constellation System

The Corvus Constellation System allows 2 to 64 microcomputers (Apple II, TRS-80, or SORCERER) to share the use of up to four 10 million-character (byte) hard disk drives. It allows each computer in the network to have open or secured access to all disk files. One computer usually becomes the monitor station for purposes of program transfer from floppy disk to hard disk and for backup from hard disk to floppy disk. An eight-computer network would use one Constellation controller and a network of 9 to 15 computers would chain two Constellation controllers. The two-to eight-computer network would look like this:

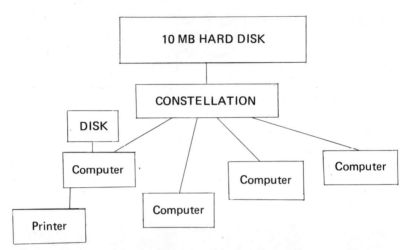

Figure 20. Corvus Constellation System Diagram

Figure 21. Corvus "Mirror" System Used To Back Up 10-Byte Hard Disk to Videocassette

The Corvus Constellation System allows:
- up to 40 million characters of storage
- sharing data between computers
- access to common data bases on the hard disk

- treatment of the hard disk drive space as if it were up to 26 different disk drives
- much more rapid disk access of programs and data
- the use of CP/M 2.0 or better as a disk operating system

The Corvus Constellation can be used with Apple II computers either as Apple DOS systems or a PASCAL system. For more information contact:

Corvus Systems, Inc.
2029 O'Toole Avenue
San Jose, CA 95131
408-946-7700
TELEX: 910-338-0226

Figure 22. Corvus Constellation System

SWTPC 6809 Time Sharing System

Southwest Technical Products Corporation (SWTPC) offers a true time-sharing microprocessor system. In this system each user uses the same computer and operates at a terminal. The SWTPC 6809 system, then, is really not a computer resource-sharing network but rather a true time-sharing system. SWTPC offers 8″ double-sided floppy disk systems, 16 million-character hard disk systems, printers, from 128K of RAM to over 700K of RAM, and a very nice low-cost terminal capable of simple graphics. Languages such as multi-user BASIC, multi-user PILOT, FORTRAN, PASCAL, and C are available. A complete relocating linking loader macro-assembler and editor are also available. The new

UNIFLEX disk operating system is similar in structure and capability to Bell Labs UNIX system for PDP11 equipment. For more information contact:
Southwest Technical Products Corporation
219 West Rhapsody
San Antonio, TX 78216
   For information on complete software support contact:
Technical Systems Consultants, Inc.
Box 2570
West Lafayette, IN 47906
317-463-2502
TELEX: 276143

CHAPTER 9

Potential Instructional and Media Center
Applications

In this chapter we will divide computer applications in the schools into two general areas—instruction and management. Different applications will be suggested and discussed.

Instruction

The area of instruction probably should be broken for the sake of discussion into three major areas:
- General Instruction
- Formal Computing
- Business Education Computing

The concerns expressed in general instruction could be applied in both formal computing and business education computing.

General Instruction

For the sake of further discussion, let us divide this area into five general types of programs:
- Games
- Drill and Practice
- Tutorials
- Simulations
- "Adventures"

Three other types of programs also exist: (1) computer-assisted instruction languages, (2) computer-manager instruction systems, and (3) information systems. What distinguishes these three from the others is that they are content-independent and allow the teacher to generate materials for use on the computer without necessarily being a programer. These were also discussed in a previous chapter.

Games on computers have been deprecated by the programing users of computers and by professional teachers. One fundamental use of games is that they help the participant gain and hone skills; they are also fun. Because they are fun, people play them again and again, constantly reinforcing their skills. Few learners like practicing skills just for the sake of practice and yet practice is needed to become skillful. Many areas of curriculum involve skill building; typical activities in these areas turn off learners. Careful analysis of the various successful computer games could provide generalized programs into which a wide variety of skill building activities could be placed. Some games provide vehicles for developing problem solving strategies or practicing a particular problem solving strategy. These games could also be effectively adapted to the curriculum. In fact, existing computer games could be examined and evaluated on their general ability to provide the opportunity to learn skill in each of the cognitive domain levels. From such an analysis one could develop general program models for games to allow skill building in:

- Acquiring knowledge
- Displaying comprehension
- Application of information to tasks
- Analysis of tasks
- Synthesis of a problem solving strategy
- Evaluation of the relative effectiveness of several problem solving strategies applied to the same problem.

These models could then be applied in various content areas.

Drill and practice programs can be very interesting and useful if several capabilities are built in:

- include the ability to give the learner immediate assessment of response
- allow the learner to specify how many problems to do
- allow the learner to select the general level of difficulty but have the drill and practice program provide a simple-to-difficult progression within that level
- keep a student profile record automatically and then allow the learner to see that profile and use it to decide on the nature of material for drill and practice.

These features give students some measure of control over how often and how much they drill and practice. The profiling capability allows the learner to compare one performance against another for purposes of self-improvement.

Tutorials typically could be used for instruction procedures and content that is constant and stable. These programs are useful in helping the learner to develop an information base in a particular content area. Tutorials are probably most easily developed through a computer-assisted instruction language such as PILOT. There are, however, a variety of tutorial programs written in

BASIC. The reasons for writing a tutorial in BASIC usually relate to the use of complex calculations and/or the use of elaborate graphics. Tutorials on microcomputers should probably:

- present information systematically and in reasonably small chunks
- require the learner to demonstrate acquisition of the key information via a question/answer procedure
- periodically require the learner to bring together several key pieces of information to deal with or solve a problem
- provide knowledge of correctness of response immediately after the learner's response and a remedial sequence if the learner's response was incorrect
- provide a summary of the important key information learned and the relationship of that information to real world problems or issues.

Tutorials, like lectures, can be dry and didactic or they can be effervescent and interesting. Usually the difference involves helping the learner to see the importance of the information in his or her immediate life or not-too-distant plans.

Simulations usually allow the learner to manipulate a data base or a mathematical model in order to see the effects of variables on the model or data base. The microcomputer allows creation of fairly complex, real, and interesting simulations of problems in the world. The Huntington Two Project under the direction of Dr. Ludwig Braun produced a series of simulations in the areas of ecology, sociology, and economics. Out of this project have come, for example:

- POP—a simulation that allows investigation of three different methods of population projection
- STERL—a simulation that investigates the effectiveness of two methods of pest control
- BUFFALO—a simulation that allows investigation of policies regarding herd management
- MALARIA—a simulation dealing with budgetary manipulation in a fight to control a malaria epidemic
- MARKET—a simulation allowing several learners individually to control the production level, advertising budget, and unit price for the products of competitive companies
- LIMITS—a simulation using a world model based on population, food supply, industrial output, and resource depletion. Six variables are available for manipulation: birth rate, death rate, industrial output, growth rate, and food production rate.

Other popular simulations include:

- HAMURABI—a simulation in which you become the adminis- trator/ruler of a city state with an economy based on the barter system. All barter is based on bushels of grain and you learn through trial and error how much to feed people, how much to plant, and how to expand the city state
- KING—a simulation of an island kingdom based on a communal treasury. As the premier of the country you make decisions on the budget and distribution of money
- FURTRADER—a simulation in which you are the leader of a French fur trading expedition in 1776. Your goal is to sell furs, buy supplies, and survive a journey to one of three forts
- CIVILWAR—a simulation based on 14 battles of the Civil War. The information presented is based on the actual occurrence. You choose for the battles an offensive strategy, a defensive strategy, and amounts spent for food, salaries, and ammunition. You are then rated comparatively against the actual strategy used for the battle.

A new breed of super-realistic simulations are showing up now. They are usually designed for a 32K to 48K system with disk which means that they can be very complex. One of the more recent of these entries is THREE MILE ISLAND which allows a realistic simulation of the famous nuclear incident.

A good simulation usually:

- allows for a variety of outcomes
- provides a rating system
- requires the learner to deduce some important facts
- provides some realistic chaotic events which have an effect on the learner's strategy
- allows a way to save the current state of a simulation and return to it later
- requires the learner to verbalize problem solving strategies.

Simulations are usually quite structured and thus performance can be readily improved by judicious note taking.

A new form of simulation has developed called an *adventure*. An adventure is an extremely flexible form of a simulation in which you control the sequences of the simulation via the use of active command sentences (usually two words) like "read note," or "go south," etc. These adventure simulations tend to be quite absorb- ing and can be designed to foster some very interesting problem solving procedures. Two interesting articles on creating adven- ture simulations are "Adventure," by Ben Moser, *Creative Com-*

puting, November 1979, 5(11), 139, and "Spelunker," by Thomas R. Mimlitch, *MCRIO,* October 1979, 17, 15-24. (This one was written for a 16K Apple II.) Adventures have tended to be pure "fantasy games" but they could just as well be modeled on some aspects of the real world and still be fascinating.

A judicious combination of all of these procedures for general education could produce some very interesting curricula.

Formal Computing

Many college and university departments of computer science now expect to receive high school students with a fair background in computer languages. For that reason the following general plan for three semesters of formal computing would be useful.

SEMESTER 1. BASIC
1. Fundamental language features
2. Data file handling
   A. Sequential files
   B. Random files
SEMESTER 2. PASCAL
1. Fundamental language features
2. Data files and data types
SEMESTER 3. COBOL
1. Fundamental language features
2. Data files and procedures

BASIC is proposed simply because it is the de facto microcomputer language. It would probably be useful if the BASIC used were Microsoft 5.0 under CP/M; students could then go right into a DEC PDP 11 series system and BASIC with very little relearning. PASCAL is proposed because it allows and encourages the development of structured programing style. COBOL is suggested because COBOL currently is the de facto business computing language. The use of all three would allow the student to begin college or work as a beginning programer or computer operator.

Business Education Computing

With the advent of truly low-cost business computing capability ranging from $4,500 to $15,000 for a complete and useful system, small businesses are bringing microcomputers in-house to perform business tasks. These tasks range from mailing-label production to inventory to financial procedures.

A two-semester sequence on small business microcomputer

application would probably resemble the following:

SEMESTER 1.
1. Word processing
2. Data base management
   A. Mail label listing
   B. Inventory
SEMESTER 2.
1. Accounts receivable systems
2. Accounts payable systems
3. General ledger systems

A graduate of such a two-semester sequence should be able to use all of the systems specified with some skill.

Media Center Applications

The potential applications list for media centers could grow almost indefinitely. We shall examine a limited set and then present a Resource list of programs useful in putting the applications into practice.

Application 1. Booking media use (reservations systems). Three useful analyses which could be generated are:
1. recommended replacement list
2. recommended acquisitions to offset volume of usage
3. recommended duplicate acquisitions based on wear and tear of existing copy

Application 2. Booking equipment (reservations system). Two useful analyses which could be generated are:
1. recommended new acquisitions based on heavy use of existing pieces
2. aged replacement list

Application 3. Equipment Repairs File. This program could:
1. track frequence of repair by piece and model
2. track for excessive repairs
3. prepare a list of commonly used parts
4. estimate costs for coming year repairs based on previous years' data

Application 4. Equipment Parts Inventory. This program would:
1. track parts used
2. record parts received
3. automatically print warning of low parts level
4. produce current inventory listing

5. produce parts used year to date and cost listing
6. produce labels for parts and/or bins

Application 5. Production Supplies Inventory. This program could:
1. track supplies used
2. record incoming supplies
3. print warning of low supplies levels
4. produce current inventory listing
5. produce supplies used year to date and cost listing
6. produce labels for supplies

Application 6. Services and Time Reservation System. Could be used for instructional development, consulting, film production, video production, etc.

Application 7. Mailing List Program

Application 8. An Encumbrance and Expenditure System. Could be useful in tracking items not received to date and estimating no-show orders

Application 9. Information Retrieval System by Selected Subject Areas.

Application 10. Project Cost Estimation. Could allow an instructional development team to project estimated project costs rapidly

Application 11. Word Processing. Could be useful in report preparation and catalog production.

Most of these applications can be implemented without programming skills using programs from the following sections.

Resources: Mailing Label Systems, Word Processing, and Data Base Systems

Mailing Label Sytem

APPLE POST
(mailing label system)   Apple Computer, Inc.
                                         10260 Bandley Drive
                                         Cupertino, CA 95014
                                         408-996-1010
Available for: APPLE II, 32K, APPLESOFTROM.
                                         2 disk drives, printer
                                         and control card

MAIL/FILE SYSTEM   Acorn Software Products, Inc.
                        634 N. Carolina Avenue, SE

	Washington, DC 20003
	202-544-4259
Available for:	TRS-80 Level II, Model I.
	expansion interface, 32K,
	disk and printer;
	TRS-80 Model II and printer

MAILING ADDRESS   Lifeboat Associates
by PEACHTREE   2248 Broadway
                       New York, NY 10024
                       212-580-0082
                       .TELEX: 220501
Available for: Unmodified CP/M.

MAILING LIST   Progressive Software
(mailing label program) P.O.Box 273
                       Plymouth Meeting, PA 19462
MAILROOM PLUS   The Peripheral People
(mailing label system) P.O.Box 524
                       Mercer Island, WA 98040
                       206-232-4505
Available for: TRS-80 Level II, Model I,
                       32K-48K expansion interface,
                       disk and printer.

M-LABEL   Computer Corner of New Jersey
(mailing label system) 439 Route 23
                       Pompton Plains, NJ 07444
                       201-835-7080
Available for: OSI C4-2P, 2 drives, printer;
                       OSI C4 MF (24K), 2 drives, printer;
                       OSI C2-8P, 2 drives, printer;
                       OSI C8P, 2 drives, printer;
                       OSI C8S/C28S.C20EM, 2 drives,
                       printer;
                       OSI C3 series, 2 drives, printer.

NAD*   Structured Systems Group
(mailing label system) 5204 Clarement
                       Oakland, CA 94618
                       415-547-1567
Available for: Unmodified CP/M.

LETTERIGHT   Structured Systems Group
(Letter writer—works   5204 Clarement
with NAD)   Oakland, CA 94618
                            415-547-1567
Note: Letteright can automatically use the NAD file for name and
address insertion in letters.
Available for: Unmodified CP/M.

POSTMASTER   Lifeboat Associates
(mailing label system)   2248 Broadway
                            New York, NY 10024
                            212-580-0082
                            TELEX: 220501

Available for: Unmodified CP/M and
                            Modified TRS-80 CP/M.

SUPER-M-List   Supersport Associates
(mailing label system)   P.O.Box 1628
                            Champaign, IL 61820
                            217-344-7596
Available for: Unmodified CP/M.

USMAIL   The Software Factory
Available for: (mailing label system)
                            23849 LaSalle Canyon Drive.
                            Newhall, CA 91321
Available for: Unmodified CP/M.

Text Editors and Word Processing

APPLE WRITER   Apple Computer, Inc.
(editor)   10260 Bandley Drive
                            Cupertino, CA 95014
                            408-996-1010
Available for: APPLE II, 48K, Disk II,
                            Printer Controller card, printer.

the CORRESPONDENT Southwestern Data Systems
(editor)   P.O.Box 582-M
                            Santree, CA 92071
                            714-562-3670

Available for: APPLE II, APPLESOFT ROM, and Disk.

CRAE   Highlands Computer Services
(co-resident editor   14422 SE 132nd
for Applesoft)   Renton, VA 98055
Available for: APPLE II, APPLESOFT ROM, 48K
                        and Disk.

DISK TEXT EDITOR   Services Unique, Inc.
and REPORT   2441 Rolling View Drive
GENERATOR   Dayton, OH 45431
(word processing
system)
Available for: APPLE II, 32K, Disk II and
                        printer

EASY WRITER   Information Unlimited Software
(word processing system) 793 Vincente St.
                        Berkeley, CA 94707
                        415-525-4046
Available for: APPLE II, 32K-48K, Disk II,

Printer desirable (and use of SUP·R·Terminal board recommended.

FORMATTER   Programma International, Inc.
(word processing—   3400 Wilshire Blvd.
formatter program to be Los Angeles, CA 90010
used with PIE Editor)   213-384-0579
                        213-384-1116
                        213-384-1117
Available for: APPLE II, 32K, Cassette and printer,
                        APPLE II, 32K, Disk II and printer.

MANUSCRIPTER   COMPUSYSTEMS
(word processing system) P.O.Box 5144
                        2301 Devine Street
                        Columbia, S.C. 29205
                        803-254-0804
                        800-854-2003 Ext 895
                        Cal. 800-522-1500 Ext 895
Available for: APPLE II, 48K Disk.

PERSONAL TEXT Charles Mann & Associates
PROCESSOR   Micro Software Division
(word processing 7594 San Remo Trail
system)   Yucca Valley, CA 92284
       714-365-9718
Available for: APPLE II, 32K (48K desirable),
       Disk II and printer.

PROGRAM LINE Synergistic Software
EDITOR   5221 120th Avenue, S.E.
(editor)   Bellevue, WA 98006
Available for: APPLE II and DISK II.

+WRITE-ON!   Rainbow Computing, Inc.
(word processing system) 9719 Reseda Blvd.
       Northridge, CA 91324
       213-349-5560
Available for: APPLE II, APPLESOFT, 32K
       and DISK II.

DISK BASED WORD Pensadoyne
PROCESSOR   4441 West First Avenue
(word processing Vancouver, B.C. V6R 449
system)   604-224-3107
Available for: TRS-80 Level II, Model I,
       expansion interface, 16K,
       disk and printer.

The ELECTRIC The Peripheral People
SECRETARY   P.O.Box 524
(word processing Mercer Island, WA 98040
system)   206-232-4505
Available for: TRS-80, Level II, Model I, 32K expansion interface, disk and printer.

SCRIPSIT   Radio Shack
(word processing system)
Available for: TRS-80, Level II, Model I, expansion interface, 32K-48K, disk and special printer.

ELECTRIC PENCIL Michael Shrayer Software, Inc.
(editor)   1198 Los Robles Drive

Palm Springs, CA 92262
714-323-1400

Available for: Unmodified CP/M, TRS-80 MOD. I
DOS, APPLE II DOS

PIE TEXT   Programma International, Inc.
EDITOR   3400 Wilshire Blvd.
Los Angeles, CA 90010
213-384-0579
213-384-1116
213-384-1117
Available for: APPLE II, 16K, Cassette, APPLE II,
32K, Disk II, TRS-80, Level II, Model
I, 16K, Cassette.

VEDIT   CompuView Products, Inc.
(editor)   1531 Jones Drive
Ann Arbor, MI 48105
313-996-1299
Available for: Unmodified CP/M, SORCERER,
TRS-80.

ZTEL   Computer Design Labs
(text editor)   342 Columbus Avenue
Trenton, NJ 98629
604-599-2146
Available for: Unmodified CP/M, Modified TRS-80,
Model I CP/M, TRS-80, Model II
CP/M, TPM.

TOP   Computer Design Labs
(word processing-   342 Columbus Avenue
formatter program)   Trenton, NJ 08629
609-599-2146
Available for: Unmodified CP/M,
Modified TRS-80, Model I CP/M,
TRS-80, Model II CP/M, TPM.

AUTOSCRIBE   MICROSOURCE
(word processing system) 1425 West 12th Place
Tempe, AZ 85281
602-894-9247
Available for: Unmodified CP/M.

MAGIC WAND   Small Business Applications, Inc.
(word processing system)   3220 Louisiana
                               Suite 205
                               Houston, TX 77006
                               713-528-5158
Available for: Unmodified CP/M.

FMT   The Software Works
(word processing—   8369 Vickers
text formatter only)   San Diego, CA 92111
                               714-569-1721
Available for: Unmodified CP/M

POLYTEXT/80   Lifeboat Associates
(word processing—   2248 Broadway
formatter only)   New York, NY 10024
                               212-580-0082
                               TELEX: 220501
Available for: Unmodified CP/M, Modified TRS-80
                               CP/M.

POLYVUE/80   Lifeboat Associates
(text editor)   2248 Broadway
                               New York, NY 10024
                               212-580-0082
                               TELEX: 220501
Available for: Unmodified CP/M, Modified TRS-80
                               CP/M.

TEXT WRITER III   Lifeboat Associates
(word processing—   2248 Broadway
formatter only)   New York, NY 10024
                               202-580-0082
                               TELEX: 220501
Available for: Unmodified CP/M, Modified TRS-80
                               CP/M.

Note: Compatible with Electric Pencil Files

TFS   Supersoft Associates
(word processing—   P.O.Box 1628

text formatter only),   Champaign, IL 61820
uses standard CPM Ed   217-344-7596
files
Available for: Unmodified CP/M.

UPDAISY   Info Soft Systems, Incorporated
(word processing system) 25 Sylvan Road South
                     Westport, XCT 06880
                     203-266-8937
Available for: Unmodified CP/M.

WORD-MASTER by   Lifeboat Associates
MICROPRO   2248 Broadway
(text editor)   New York, NY 10024
                     202-580-0082
                     TELEX: 220501
Available for: Unmodified CP/M.

WORD-STAR by   Lifeboat Associates
MICROPRO   2248 Broadway
(word processing system) New York, NY 10024
                     202-580-0082
                     TELEX: 220501
Available for: Unmodified CP/M.

Data Base Systems

CBS   Lifeboat Associates
(Database—no language 2248 Broadway
required)   New York, NY 10024
                     212-580-0082
                     TELEX: 220501
Available for: Unmodified CP/M, Modified TRS-80
                     CP/M.

CCA DATA   Personal Software
MANAGEMENT   592 Weddell Drive
SYSTEM   Sunny Vale, CA 94086
(Data Base   408-745-7841
System
Available for: APPLE II DOS, TRS-80, Model I,
                     DOS.

THE CREATOR
(generates BASIC
programs in response to
stated data needs)
Available for:

Complete Business Systems, Inc.
9420 West Foster Avenue
Chicago, IL 60656

TRS-80, Model I (DOS), TRS-80,
Model II (DOS), APPLE II (DOS).

DATA BANK
(data bank system)

Available for:

Data Access Corporation
4221 Ponce De Leon Blvd.
Coral Gables, FL 33146
305-446-0669
TRS-80, Model II.

DATABASE
MANAGEMENT
SYSTEM
(data base system)
Available for:

United Software of America
750 Third Avenue
New York, NY 10017

16-32K CBM/PET and 240 PET
DISK System (printer useful but
optional).

DATASTAR
(Data base system)

Available for:

Micropro International Corp.
1299 4th Street
San Rafael, CA 94901
415-457-8990
TELEX: 340388
Unmodified CP/M.

FILEMASTER I
FILEMASTER II
(Data base system)
Available for:

Rainbow Computing, Inc.

APPLE II, 32K, and DISK II.

HDBS
(Hierarchical data base
system)

Available for:

. Micro Data Base System, Inc/Lifeboat
Box 248
Lafayette, IN 47902
317-742-7388
Unmodified CP/M and requires
1. BASIC-80 or
2. COMPILED
    A. BASIC-80
    B. FORTRAN-80 or

3. COBOL-80
4. MACRO-80.

ISAM-DS   Decision Systems
(Data Based System—set P.O.Box 13006
of routines for data base Denton, TX 76203
creation)
Available for: APPLE II, 32K, APPLESOFT ROM,
                             and DISK II.

MAGSAM   Micro Applications Group
(data base system)   7300 Caldus Avenue
                             Van Nuys, CA 91606
Available for: Unmodified CPM and requires
                             1. CBASIC 2 or
                             2. MICROSOFT BASIC or
                                MICROPOLIS BASIC.

MDBS   Micro Data Base Systems/Lifeboat
(full network data base)   Box 248
                             Lafayette, IN 47902
                             317-742-7388
Available for: Unmodified CP/M and requires
                             1. BASIC-80 or
                             2. COMPILED
                                A. BASIC-80
                                B. FORTRAN-80 or
                             3. COBOL-80
                             4. MACRO-80.

MODIFIABLE DATA   Synergistic Software
BASE   5221 120th Avenue, SE
(customizable data base Bellevue, WA 98006
system)   206-641-1917
Note: This data base program modifies itself based on your
answers to its questions.
Available for: APPLE II, 48K, and DISK II.

PEARL (Level I, II, III) Computer Pathways Unlimited, Inc.
(data base creator   2151 Davcor Street, S.E.
system)   Salem, OR 97302
                             503-363-8929

Note: This software system generates a data base program based upon your answers to questions.
Available for: Unmodified CP/M.

SELECTOR III-C2   Lifeboat Associates
(Database—requires   2248 Broadway
CBASIC-2)   New York, NY 10024
212-580-0082
TELEX: 220501
Available for: Unmodified CP/M, Modified TRS-80
CP/M.

WHATSIT   Computer Headware
(self-indexing query   Box 14694
system)   San Francisco, CA 94114
Available for: APPLE II, DOS, TRS-80, Model I
DOS.

CHAPTER 10

Microcomputers in Education

Rather than attempt to survey all school- and education-selected computer projects we shall describe a representative series of projects ranging over many educational levels, including:
- the elementary school
- gifted learner programs
- summer computer camp
- statewide educational computing network
- special grants for personal computers in education
- education for the deaf
- dissemination project
- private sector education
- commercial training
- medical education

The projects and programs are cited because they represent an interesting conceptual approach to the business of developing computer literacy.

The Elementary School

Ellen Richman, an Ohio elementary teacher, developed a research project titled "Computers in the Classroom—A Curriculum for Grades 4-8." As a result she developed a computer literacy course which she provides under independent contract to schools in Ohio. As an itinerant teacher, she moves from school to school, as do shared music and foreign language teachers at the elementary school level. The major difference is that Richman is independent and supplies her own microcomputer.

Her class format includes 18 hours of formal instruction and 18 hours of laboratory activity with the computer. Each student gets to write and run a program on the computer. Using one computer, classes are divided into two or three lab sessions to allow all students to participate.

The students are asked to create files of articles on computers, and they discuss real life applications and the ethics of computer usage. The course climaxes with a computer fair (a sort of show-

and-tell session) for parents. For more information contact:
Ellen Richman
245 Meadow Lane
Moreland Hills, OH 44022

Another shuttle type program, called the Science Shuttle, is operated by the Lawerence Hall of Science, University of California, Berkeley. The Science Shuttle programs take a dozen microcomputers by van to area schools. The goal of the program are:

- to give a large number of students the opportunity to experiment with computers
- to bring microcomputers into all classrooms, not just computer curriculum classrooms.

The Science Shuttle programs provide about 5,000 contact hours per year. For more information contact:
Joyce Hakansson
Coordinator, Computer Education
Lawerence Hall of Science
University of California
Berkeley, CA 94720
415-642-3167

The Dallas Public Schools have developed a complete microcomputer based Kindergarten-through-eighth-grade mathematics program. The entire program is cassette-based with the programs prepared in BASIC. The program covers:

- addition
- subtraction
- numeration
- multiplication
- division
- decimals
- fractions.

The program has been released for purchase. For more information contact:
Foundation for Quality Education
5217 Ross Avenue
Dallas, TX 75206

Gifted Programs

The Jefferson Lighthouse School offers a program for gifted and talented youngsters at the third and fourth grade level. The children receive about 45 minutes a week in formal instruction. The

major concerns developed in the program include:
- developing a perspective on computers and their abilities
- developing an understanding of how computers use instructions to do a task
- developing some skills in communicating with a computer (the medium is BASIC)
- developing creative program solutions to problems
- speculating on future uses of computers.

For more information contact:
Sally Greenwood Larsen
1643 LaSalle Street
Racine, WI 53404

Summer Computer Camp

Michael Zabinski has developed a summer day camp with computer emphasis to provide children with the opportunity to deal with both recreational and instructional applications of computers. The outcome should be a suitable basis for extended computer study in a formal school setting. The objectives are:
- introduce computer concepts and techniques and thus provide a general appreciation of the power and limitations of computers; i.e., to remove the mystique about computers
- provide a technical, social, and moral perspective on present and future roles of computers in our society
- acquire some competence in computer operations and programing in BASIC, without attempting to develop exceptionally proficient programers
- use the computer as a motivational instrument to stimulate interest in science and mathematics. Because of the step-by-step approach, techniques gained from using the computer may be applied to life situations
- discover that working with a computer can be recreational and entertaining
- provide a new learning experience that includes such topics as flowcharting, programing, algorithms, modeling, hardware, software, and library programs.

For more information contact:
Michael P. Zabinski
Fairfield University
North Benson Road
Fairfield, CT 06430

Statewide Computing Network

The Minnesota Educational Computing Consortium (MECC) was created in 1972 in response to the need for centralized coordination and planning to provide all state educational institutions with equal opportunity for access to computational facilities. Members include the Minnesota State University System, the University of Minnesota, the Minnesota Community College System, the Minnesota Department of Education (representing 436 school districts), and the Minnesota Department of Administration. The MECC time-share system serves over 1,000 terminals.

MECC created a task force to survey the field of microcomputers, analyze their capabilities, disseminate information on microcomputers, and develop recommendations concerning a large scale purchase plan for an appropriate and useful microcomputer system.

The minimum educational system was defined as including:
1. a microprocessor (8- or 16-bit)
2. a keyboard and printer or keyboard and video display
3. an ASCII input (keyboard)
4. random access mass storage
5. a manufacturer- or vendor-supplied operating system
6. the BASIC language
7. at least 12K of *user* RAM
8. complete system and language documentation.

The result was a statewide contract for the purchase of 32K disk-based Apple II systems with color monitor.

The analysis report of the survey is interesting and necessary reading for those with responsibility for purchasing microcomputers. For more information contact:
MECC Instructional Services Division
2520 Broadway Drive
Lauderdale, MN 55113

Special Grants

The Apple Company has established the Apple Education Foundation as a national nonprofit corporation designed to "support and develop new methods of learning through the use of small computers." As a result the Apple Education Foundation has given the following grants:
PASCAL-Based Interactive Statistics and Physics Materials ,

Dr. Alfred Bork, University of California, Irvine

Microcomputer-Based Education Environmental Control for Severely Handicapped Children, I. Laefsky, University of Pennsylvania

Classroom and Lecture Hall Use of Microcomputers in Mathematics, Dr. L.A. Karlovitz, Georgia Institute of Technology

Evaluation of CAI for Patient Education in Low-Income Community Clinics, Dr. Lynda Ellis, University of Minnesota, Laboratory Medicine and Pathology

Multi-Model Approach to Learning Disabilities, Marguerite Mason, Eastern Illinois Special Education, Mattoon, Illinois

Problem Solving Simulations Using Microcomputers in Nursing Education, Allen M. Villiers, Texas Women's University, College of Nursing, Dallas, Texas

Museum Exhibits—Enhanced by Stand-Alone Computers, Dr. E.C. VanRennes, Cranbrook Institute of Science, Bloomfield Hills, Michigan

Color-Coded Initial Reading Program, Robert S. Houghton, Wales Elementary School, Wales, Wisconsin

High Resolution Graphics in College Mathematics, Dr. Thomas Wallgren, Milliken University, Decatur, Illinois

Instructional Computing Training Materials for Rehabilitation Facility Administrators, Dr. Keith Gardner, University of San Francisco, San Francisco, California

Mathematical Graphing Courseware for Micro-computers, Dr. John D. Kelley, Albany Jr. College, Albany, Georgia

Adult Core Curriculum Educational Delivery Systems for Use in Henry Ford Hospital and Detroit Motor Car Plants, Dr. E.C. Hertzler, University of Michigan, Dearborn, Michigan

Computer Software for High School Physics Instruction, Dr. John Finnessey, Marshall Town Community Schools, Marshall Town, Iowa

Computer Assisted Interview Evaluation, Dr. Wayne R. Waller, University of Southern California, School of Dentistry, Los Angeles, California

Individualized Criterion-Referenced Reading Test and Site Word Acquisition in Early Reading, Dr. Richard Cummins, University of Montana, Missoula, Montana

Microcomputer Instruction for Early Learning, Dr. Ann Piestrup, Advanced Learning Technology, Woodside, California

For applications for grants or information contact:
Apple Education Foundation, Inc.

20605 Lazaneo Drive
Cupertino, CA 95014

Education for the Deaf

The California School for the Deaf has begun an intensive learning program with the use of microcomputers. The program has two goals:

1. to test whether students learn more effectively with the aid of microcomputers
2. to establish the California School for the Deaf (CSD) as a regional center for the development and distribution of lessons.

The school will score on the Stanford Achievement Test (with norms for the deaf) for students learning with microcomputers compared to students learning by more traditional means. Their program has developed over the years with some assistance from the staff of the Lawerence Hall of Science computer group.

The staff at CSD has completed development and testing of a math program for all grades and a language program. The technical staff has developed general purpose lesson programs to which the content specialist adds the appropriate content. For further information contact:

Geoff Zawolkow
Coordinator, Computer-Assisted Instruction
2601 Warring Street
Berkeley, CA 94704

Dissemination Project

CONDUIT is an organization formed to disseminate computer programs for learning. It was originated through National Science Foundation funding. CONDUIT has prepared a BASIC Guide for developing BASIC programs which will then be transferred to various microcomputers using a variety of dialects of the language BASIC. CONDUIT also publishes *Computers in Undergraduate Teaching: 1977 CONDUIT State of the Art Reports for Selected Disciplines* and a user newsletter called *Pipeline*.
The programs available from CONDUIT cover a major part of the curriculum and are available for TRS-80, Apple II, and PET.

CONDUIT actively solicits programs for undergraduate instruction which could usefully be distributed to the public. For

more information contact:
CONDUIT
Iowa City, Iowa

Private Sector Education

The Marin Computer Center is a nonprofit educational enterprise designed to place the effects of advanced technology within the domain of everyone. In a sense the Marin Computer Center resembles a high class "storefront computer center." It is located in the library of a modern school with carpeting and plants.

The main goal of the Marin Computer Center is to "introduce people of all ages to computers and the advanced technology which they represent in order that anyone might begin participating in the process of computer assistance for society."

MCC provides a place for families to get together and investigate computers, computer games, and computer literacy in general. For more information contact:
David or Annie Fox
Marin Computer Center
70 Skyview Terrace, Room 301
San Rafael, CA 94903

Commercial Training

Sears Laboratories of Sears and Roebuck is devoted to testing and evaluating consumer products. They have begun to use microcomputers to provide inservice employee education. They provide programing classes and allow class participants to take the microcomputers home for further study. The results have been interesting; not only do the employees learn but they are quick to see applications of the microcomputer to their specific areas of work.

The applications of the microcomputers in the day-to-day work of Sears Laboratories are truly fascinating. For more information contact:
Eugene Ostap
Senior Staff Assistant
Technical Studies
Sears Laboratories
Chicago, IL

Medical Education

Milliken Communications Corporation has developed and maintains a Continuing Medical Education Courseward Library covering urology, medicine, surgery, and psychiatry.

The material has been approved by the appropriate medical boards and CME credit is available with completion of the courses. For more information contact:

Milliken Communications Corporation
1100 Research Boulevard
St. Louis, MO 63132
1-800-325-4136

Futureworld: Education

The developments surveyed above are only examples of many projects currently under way. Several notions are of interest for speculation; the future of learning and education may well be found in:

- "storefront" microcomputer centers
- home learning courses via microcomputers
- development of materials for the talented and gifted for home use on microcomputers
- microcomputers learning and reference programs on basic survival skills for adults for home use or public office use
- home study materials for job retraining or advancement for home use on microcomputers
- local software libraries may well develop with materials for sale and/or rent.

These possibilities have an 80% or better probability of occurring on a broad-scale basis over the next 5 years.

NOTE: The information presented in this chapter has been gleaned from the following publications and references.

Apple Education News, Issue 2, February 1980. (Apple Computer Company).

A Dozen Apples for the Classroom, Joyce Hakansson and Leslie Roach, *Creative Computing*, Vol. 5, No. 9, September 1979, pp. 52-54.

Have Computer Will Travel, Ellen Richman, *Creative Computing*, Vol. 5, No. 9, September 1979, pp. 56-57.

The Marin Computer Center: A "New Age" Learning Environment,

David and Annie Fox, *Creative Computing*, Vol. 5, No. 4, April 1979, pp. 116-118.

PIPELINE, Summer 1979, (CONDUIT).

Statewide Educational Computer Systems: The Many Considerations, Kevin Hausmann, *Creative Computing*, Vol. 5, No. 9, September 1979.

CHAPTER 11

Special Applications: Electronic Mail, Networks, and Videodiscs

In recent years interest has developed in information networking, electronic mail, and home information systems. TELETEXT and VIEWDATA, systems developed in England for home information accessing,—have aroused interest in the United States. The French have also developed a system for home information accessing.

Home Information Access Systems

Home information access deals with the concept of providing access from the home through television receivers to large information bases. These information bases are primarily text-oriented but can allow some graphics and provide for limited interaction. In some cases a limited version of "computer-assisted instruction" can also be provided. The general procedure involves sending video information to the home receiver during the vertical blanking interval. The information is sent as a page of text and/or graphic information and can be in color. The home video receiver (TV) is modified to display the blanking interval video information as well as the regular broadcast television signals. The choice of video to be viewed is entirely the viewer's and can in fact be switched back and forth while watching programs. The user's television set modification also permits a choice of pages of information to view. Home information accessing systems which use this procedure are subsumed under the generic TELETEXT.

The alternative involves transmitting video information through telephone cables to an adapted television receiver. Viewers use a calculator-like selection device to call for pages of information. Home information access systems which use this approach are generically referred to as VIEWDATA systems. In Britain the VIEWDATA system carries not only information but also paid advertising. The TELETEXT system transmits its signals over the broadcast system; in Britain this is a public service and carries no paid advertising.

In the United States, the user of a TELETEXT-like system

113

could switch to the information system during commercials, causing legitimate concern for revenue supporting television services. Presumably advertising could also be sold on the TELETEXT-type system.

In the United States, the Knight-Rider newspaper group is field-testing a VIEWDATA-type system in Miami, Florida. The system is called VIEWTRON. Two television stations—KNOX-TV of St. Louis and KSL-TV of Salt Lake City—have developed and are testing demonstration systems based on the TELETEXT concept. Micro-Text of Philadelphia seems to have developed a TELETEXT-like system for use on cable television systems as well as broadcast stations. The page shown typically can contain 32 characters per row and 20 rows per page for a total of 640 characters per page.

Although the VIEWDATA and TELETEXT systems are useful in their own right, microcomputer inter-connection possibilities are not being developed for them at present.

The most applicable information accessing scheme for microcomputers lies in the area of electronic mail, computer bulletin board systems, computer-based teleconferencing, and accessing large time-share computers and their associated data bases. One of the most widely known of the access-to-time-share systems was the Apple II-Dow Jones Industrial Averages arrangement. With a telephone coupler (modem or acoustic coupler) and the Apple II it is possible to access the Dow Jones data base and transfer data through telephone lines to your machine. Once the data is in your machine, you can save it on disk for further use.

Recently, access to several time-sharing systems has become possible for home microcomputers. These systems are:
• The Source
• MICRONET
• EDUNET
• The Handicapped Educational Exchange.

The Source, the first home consumer information in the U.S., was started in June 1979. It is available through:
Telecomputing Corporation of America
1616 Anderson Road
McLean, VA 22101
The Source provides access to:
• a version of the UPI newswire service
• the New York Times Information Bank (a bibliographic

service)
- electronic mail procedures
- analyses based on the Wall Street index.

These services are provided by transmissions through both TYMNET and TELENET.

MICRONET is a computer network designed for personal computer access in much the same manner as the Source. It operates through:

Personal Computing Division
CompuServe Incorporated
5000 Arlington Centre Blvd.
Columbus, OH 43220

MICRONET provides access to:
- electronic mail
- file editing and manipulation
- business programs
- computing languages
- a stock price index service
- programs which can be transferred to your home computer and charged to your credit card.

The services are available by long distance call or TYMNET in selected cities.

EDUNET is a national educational information network established by the EDUCOM organization. It is unusual in that it does not own any computer facilities but rather provides an organizational framework permitting various colleges, universities, and other teaching institutions to share resources. EDUNET consists of 15 different colleges and universities with 23 host computers. Users may access these host computers through networks such as TELENET and TYMNET. EDUNET resources include:
- computer-assisted instruction
- CAI author languages
- planning and analysis models
- simulation languages and games
- extensive data bases
- data base management systems
- information retrieval systems
- teleconferencing
- electronic mail.

EDUNET has a hotline and also publishes a quarterly newsletter, the *EDUNET News*. The address for EDUNET is:

EDUNET
P.O. Box 364
Princeton, NJ 08540
Aspects of EDUCOM, the parent organization, have been funded
through National Science Foundation grants and grants from the
Lilly Endowment.

The Handicapped Educational Exchange is a computer information retrieval system designed for use by handicapped persons

*Figure 23. Texas Instruments TI 99/4 Microcomputer
RS-232-C Interface*

both for communications and education. The exchange, called HEX, is being funded by the Federal Bureau of Education for the handicapped. It is based on a microcomputer system with two large-size floppy disk drives. Communications can be via the standard ASCII terminal systems or the older BAUDOT terminals used in programs for the deaf. HEX is sponsored by The Amateur Radio Research and Development Corporation (AMRAD). For information contact:

Paul Rinaldo
1524 Springvale Ave.
McLean, VA 22101
703-356-8919

Figure 24. Commodore CBM/PET Acoustic Coupler (Modem)

The system is relatively new and its dial-up number is 703-281-2222.

To communicate with an information network, you need:
- a microcomputer with an RS-232-C interface
- an acoustic coupler or modem
- a program to allow your terminal to function as an intelligent terminal or a nonintelligent terminal.

When your computer functions as a nonintelligent terminal it merely (1) receives and sends data and (2) displays the data on its videoscreen. No other functions are usable.

When your computer functions as an intelligent terminal you can:
- send data from the keyboard
- display incoming information on your videoscreen
- save the incoming data to disk
- get a data file from disk and transmit it in its entirety to the host computer.

The following Resources section lists some of the available terminal programs. See the chapter on special accessories for acoustic couplers.

Resources: Terminal Programs

The Apple Communication Transfer System (ACTS) terminal program with data transfer)
Available for:

NEO/ABB5
P. O. Box 4731
Cleveland, OH 44126

APPLE II,
APPLESOFT ROM,
16K, DISK II, and D. C.
Hayes Micromodem.

DATA CAPTURE 3.0

(terminal program)

SOUTHEASTERN SOFTWARE
7270 Culpepper Drive
New Orleans, LA 70126
504-246-8438
504-246-7937

Figure 25. Texas Instruments TI 99/4 Acoustic Coupler (Modem)

Available for: APPLE II,
                                              APPLESOFT ROM, &
                                              DISK II.

QS Smart Terminal   Quality Software
(terminal program)   6660 Reseda Blvd.,
                                              Suite 202
                                              Reseda, CA 91335
                                              213-344-6599

Available for: SORCERER, 16K,
                                              Cassette.

SMARTTERM   MICRON, INC.
(terminal program)   10045 Waterford Drive
                                              Elicott City, MD 21043
                                              301-461-2721

Available for: TRS-80 Level II Model
                                              I, expansion interface,
                                              disk, RS 232 C
                                              interface.

TEKTRONIC 4010 EMULATOR   APPLE II
   The ABW Corporation has produced a ROM-based conversion
for the APPLE II microcomputer which allows the APPLE to act
as if it were a TEKTRONIC 4010 graphics system. It capitalizes
on the high-resolution mode of APPLE graphics and allows use of
multicolored displays, standard video output, and the use of selec-
tive erasing of the graphics image.
ABW Corporation
Box M 1047
Ann Arbor, MI 48106
313-971-9364

TERMCOM   STATCOM CORP.
(interface for communication   Suite 202
capabilities)   5758 Balcones Drive
                                              Austin, TX 78731
                                              512-451-0221

Available for: TRS-80Model I.

TERMINAL   Miller Microcomputer
(modifications for Radio Shack   Services
terminal program)   61 Lake Shore Road
                                              Natick, WA 01760
                                              617-653-6136

Available for: TRS-80 Level II Model
I, expansion interface,
32K, disk, RS 232 C
interface and optionally
the modem.

TIELINE   PROGRAMMA INTERNATIONAL
(terminal program)   3400 Wilshire Blvd.
Los Angeles, CA 90010
213-384-0579
213-384-1116
213-384-1117
Available for: TRS-80 Level II Model I, 32K, RS
232 C interface, expansion interface,
DOS 2.1, and acoustic coupler (CAY
modem recommended; Also
TRS-80-modem).

ST-80D   The Software Exchange
(terminal program with   6 South Street
data transfer)   Box 68
Milford, NH 03055
800-258-1790
Available for: TRS-80 Level II Model I, expansion
interface, 32K, RS 232 C interface
and disk.

ST-80I*   Houston Micro-Computer
(terminal program—set   5313 Bissonet
serial board from   Bellaire, TX 77401
keyboard, auto line feed   713-661-2005
and line printer on)

ST-80II*
(terminal program—dump memory
to disk, lower case, auto log
on, send buffer to serial
output port, serial input to
memory)

ST-80III*
(terminal program—help

command auto answer/auto
originate, warm reset, job log)

Available for: TRS-80 Model I Level II, expansion
                                    interface, disk, printer, RS 232 C,
                                    acoustic coupler (modem).

Videodisks

For some time now videodisks have loomed on the horizon,
promising tremendous potential for education. Positive aspects of
videodisks include:
• Videodisks cost less in raw materials
• The playback equipment is potentially less expensive to
  purchase
• Videodisk players should be less expensive to maintain and
  potentially they can present both single frame video and motion
  video.
On the negative side, the production costs of enough material to fill
a videodisk could make it very expensive to the user.

Videodisks have the following characteristics:
• About 54,000 video frames on each side
• 30 minutes of motion in linear play mode
• 60 minutes of motion in constant linear velocity mode
• possibly 7.5 million bytes or characters of computer program
  storage
• up to four audio channels
At least nine manufacturers are experimenting with developmental models of videodisk players. Of this group, apparently only
two have developed units that can both record and play videodisks.
Only two currently offer models sufficiently flexible to be interfaced to a microcomputer for educational purposes. One of those,
the MCA Videodisk System, has been almost universally chosen
for interfacing experiments. Such a model currently costs around
$5,000—a very expensive accessory.

Specific useful characteristics of the MCA industrial/educa-
tional videodisk system include:
• random access within 2.5 seconds to any videoframe
• stop motion
• variable slow motion

- rapid scan
- dual audio channels
- ability to be interfaced to a microcomputer

Table 1 presents some characteristics of nine of the known videodisk players and shows which microcomputers have been interfaced to videodisk players. These are still developmental systems; it would probably be somewhat difficult to acquire the appropriate interface to attach a videodisk player to your microcomputer.

If the final cost of videodisks, complete with visual information recorded on them is relatively low, then the combination of videodisk player and microcomputer can produce an almost ideal teaching/learning machine. Several experimental projects have interfaced the videodisk player to a microcomputer so that it could be controlled through a language such as BASIC or PILOT.

| | STYLUS READ | LASER READ | INTERNAL MICRO-PROCESSOR FOR RANDOM ACCESS | INTERFACED TO VIDEODISC | | | | | | HOME MODEL | INDUSTRIAL/ EDUCATION MODEL | WRITE AND READ CAPABILITY |
				APPLE II	TRS-80	SORCERER	CBM/PET	ATARI 800	TI 99/4			
MAGNAVISION		X								X		
THOMPSON CST		X	X								X	
HITACHI		X								X		
MCV VIDEODISC		X	X	X	X						X	
RCA SELECTAVISION	X									X		
JVC	X									X		
MATSUSHITA	X									X		
AEG-TELEFUNKEN	X									X		
PHILLIPS DATA SYSTEM											X	X

Table 1. Videodisc Characteristics and Usage With Microcomputers

Some Videodisk Projects*

1. BYU—Brigham Young University. Edward Schneider has directed efforts toward interfacing an MCA industrial videodisk player to microcomputers. The MCA images are displayed on one screen and the computer video information on a second screen.

2. *Control Data Corporation.* Control Data has successfully interfaced a videodisk to a single screen display using one of their experimental color PLATO terminals. This allows superimposition of PLATO text and graphics over moving or still images. The PLATO terminals developed by Control Data use the standard television screen technology rather than the original PLATO plasma displays.

3. *Hazeltine Corporation.* Hazeltine, the marketing organization for the TICCIT computer-based instructional saystem, is investigating the use of videodisk players in the TICCIT system. The main purpose if random access to videoframes and sequences.

4. *Nebraska Educational Television Network.* Rodney Daynes developed a project to interface a TRS-80 Model I microcomputer to an MCA industrial videodisk player. A series of eight videodisks for use in various content areas is being developed. Of special interest is the use of closed captions.

5. *Lister Hill National Library of Medicine.* Chuck Goldstein has a series of three videodisk projects under way: (1)Development of the Intelligent Device Controller to interface microcomputers to videodisk players; (2) interfacing the videodisk player to a PLATO terminal; and (3) investigation of the potential for storing computer programs and data on videodisks.

---

*This section presents some interesting videodisk projects and key developments. The data presented here may be found in greater detail in "Video-disk Technology in Education: The Current Scene" by Paul F. Merrill and Junius L. Bennion in the *NSPI Journal* (Nov. 1979), 18-26.

CHAPTER 12

Resources: Journals and Magazines

Many journals and magazines are available to help the aspiring microcomputer user. Some are quite technical, some deal with business concerns, some deal primarily with software at a detailed level, some deal with educational concerns in a general way, and some treat the area of personal applications. There are monthly, bimonthly, and quarterly periodicals, the print quality ranging from pulp base paper to slick stock in multiple colors. A few journals and magazines are distributed in cassette or disk form readable by a specific brand of microcomputer. An advantage of this approach is that programs listed are usually directly runnable.

These resource journals and magazines have been divided into two sections: (1) general journals and magazines and (2) machine-specific journals and magazines. In the latter category, the journal or magazine is usually devoted to a particular brand of machine or, in some rare cases, to a particular microcomputer chip; e.g., 6502. The "Focus" column provided for the general journals shows what the general tendency is for a publication.

The resource lists are as complete as possible but each month seems to bring forth a new journal or magazine.

General Journals and Magazines

Key to letters in "Focus" column:
    H = hardware emphasis—technical
    S = software/program emphasis
    B = business emphasis
    P = personal computer applications
    E = education emphasis Focus

H,S   *BYTE: The Small Systems Journal*
       McGraw-Hill
       70 Main Street
       Peterborough, NH 03458
       $18/yr., $2 newstand

E,P *Creative Computing*
Creative Computing Press
Box 789-M
Morristown, NJ 07960
15/yr., $2 newstand

E,P.S *Calculators/Computers*
DYMAX
P.O. Box 3120, Dept. 42
Menlo Park, CA 94025
$12/yr.—12 issues

E *The Computing Teacher*
Computing Center
Eastern Oregon State College
La Grande, OR 97850
$10/yr., 7 issues
Note. This journal is published by the International
Council for Computers in Education and is aimed at the
pre-college level.

S,H *Dr. Dobb's Journal of Computer Calisthenics and
Orthodontia*
People's Computer Co.
Box E, 1263 El Camino Real
Menlo Park, CA 94025
$15/yr., $2 newstand

H,S, *Kiloband Microcomputing*
B,E, 1001001 Inc.
Pine Street
Petersborough, NH 03458
$18/yr., $2.50 newstand

S,B,P *Interface Age*
McPheters, Wolfe and Jones
16704 Marguardt Avenue
Cerritos, CA 90701
$18/yr., $2 newstand

P,E,B *Personal Computing*
Benwill Publishing Corp.
1050 Commonwealth Avenue
Boston, MA 02215
$14/yr., $2 newstand

E,P,S   *Recreational Computing*
        People's Computer Co.
        Box E
        Menlo Park, CA 94025
        $10/yr., $2 newstand

P,S   *Robert Purser's Magazine*
        Robert Purser
        P.O. Box 466
        El Dorado, CA 95623
        Note: The Winter 1980 issue contains a software direc-
        tory for TRS-80, Apple II, PET and ATARI.

Machine-Specific Journals and Magazines

APPLE
APPLESEED
Softside Publication
6 South Street
Milford, NH 03055
603-673-5144
$15/12 issues

THE APPLE SHOPPE (based on applications and technique)
Apple Shoppe
P.O. Box 7101
Placentia, CA 92670
714-996-0441
$12/8 issues

COMPUTE (APPLE, PET)
Compute
P.O. Box 5119
Greensboro, NC 27403
919-272-4867
$9/6 issues

Micro; The 6502 Journal
Micro
Chelmsford, MA
$15/yr. subscription

NIBBLE
NIBBLE
Box 325
Lincoln MA 01773
$15/8 issues

SOFTSIDE: APPLE
Softside Publications
6 South Street
Milford, NH 03055
603-673-5144
$15/12 issues

TRS-80

THE ALTERNATE SOURCE
1806 Ada
Lansing, MI 48910
$9/6 issues, $2 newstand

CLOAD (a cassette-based magazine)
Box 1267
Goleta, CA 93017
$36/yr.—12 issues on cassette for TRS-80

80 MICROCOMPUTING
1001001 Inc.
Pine Street
Peterborough, NH 03458
603-924-3873/4
$15/12 issues, $40/3 yrs.

80 SOFTWARE CRITIQUE
80 Software Critique
P.O. Box 134
Waudegan, IL 60085
$24/yr./quarterly

80-US (The TRS-80 Users Journal)
80-US Journal
P.O. Box 7112
Tacoma, WA 98407
206-759-9642
$16/6 issues, $31/2 yrs., $45/3 yrs., $3 newstand

PROG/80
Softside Publications
6 South Street
Milford, NH 03055
603-673-5144
$15/12 issues

SOFTSIDE: S-80
Softside Publications
6 South Street
Milford, NH 03055
603-673-5144
$18/12 issues

T-PAL
The Mail Mart
San Francisco, CA
$24/yr., $1 for sample

TRS-80 Computing (nonprofit newsletter)
Computer Information Exchange
San Luis Rey, CA
$15/yr.

TRS-80 Monthly Newsletter
Computronics Inc.
Box 149
New York, NY 10956
$24/yr., $4 single issue

The TRS-80 Notebook
The TRS-80 Notebook
R.R. #3
Nazareth, PA 18064
$14/yr., 12 issues

ATARI

IRIDIS (for cassette magazine for ATARI)
IRIDIS
Box 550
Goleta, CA 93017
$14.95/4 issues

SOFTSIDE: ATARI
Softside Publications
6 South Street
Milford, NH 03055
603-673-5144
$15/12 issues

PET

PET: Cursor
Cursor
Goleta, CA
$33/yr., $3.95/single

OSI (Ohio Scientific)

AARDVARK/Journal for OSI
AARDVARK Technical Services
1690 Bolton
Walled Lake, MI 48088
313-624-6316

PEEK (65) (the unofficial Ohio Scientific User's Journal)
PEEK (65)
62 Southgate Avenue
Annapolis, MD 21401
$8/12 issues

HEATHKIT

BUSS (Heath kit computers)
BUSS
325-B Pennsylvania Ave. S.E.
Washington, D.C. 20003
$8.75/yr.

CHAPTER 13

Resources: Languages, Disk Operating Systems, Editor/Assemblers, and Utilities

The most flexible and useful microcomputer systems tend to be those with disk capability. Usually the manufacturer of the computer or the disk system makes available a disk operating system and a language (usually BASIC) which can load or save programs and create and access data files. It is not normally possible to read data or programs from an Apple II to a TRS-80 or a SORCERER or a PET (or vice versa) using the manufacturer's supplied disk operating system. Perhaps just as important, there are usually differences in programing capability from BASIC to BASIC. Only in computer systems sharing a common disk operating system can you reasonably expect to carry programs and/or data on disk from brand A computer to brand B. The "common" disk operating system is CP/M. Not all CP/M disk operating systems are equal, though. Some are modified to deal with internal design differences in the various microcomputers.

If you want to use a different language, disk operating system, or both, what are your options? The rest of this chapter is divided into four resource lists: (1) available languages, (2) available disk operating systems, (3) editor/assembler systems, and (4) utility programs to extend the usefulness of your microcomputer system. Please bear in mind that these resources are in addition to those supplied by your microcomputer manufacturer.

Languages

ALGOL
ALGOL—60

Lifeboat Associates
2248 Broadway
New York, NY 10024
212-580-0082
TELEX 66 8585

Available for: Unmodified CP/M.

131

APL (Interpreter—A Programing Language)

APL (based on the IBM APL language; and contains a limited subset features)	The Software Exchange P.O. Box 68 Milford, NH 03055
Available for:	TRS-80 Model I Level II, 32K (48K recommended), expansion interface and disk drive.

BASIC INTERPRETERS
(Beginners All purpose Symbolic Instruction Code)

BASIC-80 INTERPRETER	Microsoft 10800 NE 8th, Suite 819 Bellevue, WA 98004 206-455-8080 TELEX 32 8945
Available for:	Unmodified CP/M, Modified TRS-80 CP/M (1. Disk Format) (2. Memory Allocation), Modified APPLE Z-80 CP/M (Disk Format).
Basic I (Interpreter—7 digit precision)	Computer Design Labs 342 Columbus Avenue Trenton, NJ 08629 609-599-2146
Available for:	Unmodified CP/M;Modified TRS-80 Model I CP/M; TRS-80 Model II CP/M;TPM
BASIC II (Interpreter—12 digit precision)	Computer Design Labs 342 Columbus Avenue Trenton, NJ 08629 609-599-2146
Available for:	Unmodified CP/M; Modified TR-80 Model I CP/M; TRS-80 Model II CP/M; TPM.

Softside: S-80

BUSINESS BASIC (Interpreter—12 digit precision plus random access files)	Computer Design Labs 342 Columbus Avenue Trenton, NJ 08629 609-599-2146

Available for: Unmodified CP/M; Modified
TRS-80 Model I CP/M;
TRS-80 Model II CP/M;
TPM

LEVEL III BASIC   Microsoft
Available for: Cassette Based TRS-80 MOD I Level
II.

PBASIC-DS   Decision Systems
(Structured Basic   P.O. Box 13006
interpreter)   Denton, TX 76203
Available for: APPLE II, 32K, APPLESOFT
ROM, and DISK II.

TBASIC   Tarbell Electronics
(Basic interpreter)   950 Doolen Place Suite B
Carson, CA 90746
213-538-4251
213-538-2254
This BASIC has several interesting features. It allows labeling of
lines rather than line numbering. It allows procedures and varia-
bles to be local to the procedure. These features can be very useful.
Available for: Unmodified CP/M (source for this
BASIC is also available on disk)

Basic Compilers (*Beginners All purpose Symbolic Instruction Code)*

BASIC COMPILER   Topaz Programing
P.O. Box 80545
San Diego, CA 92138
Available for: Unmodified CP/M.

BASIC COMPILER   Microsoft
10800 NE 8th, Suite 819
Bellevue, WA 98004
206-455-8080
TELEX 32 8945
Available for: Unmodified CP/M; Modified TRS-80
CP/M;TRS-80 MOD I DOS.

BASEX
(a BASIC-like
intermediate compiler
language)
Available for:

Interactive Microware, Inc.
Box 771
State College, PA 16801
814-238-8294
Unmodified CP/M.

CBASIC-2
(Semicompiler)

Available for:

Lifeboat Associates
2248 Broadway
New York, NY 10024
Unmodified CP/M; Modified TRS-80
CP/M.

SBASIC (Ultimate
Computer Systems
(a structured BASIC
compiler)
Available for:

313 Meadow Lane
Hastings, MI 49058
616-945-5334

Unmodified CP/M; TRS-80 Model I
DOS.

Tiny Comp
(a tiny BASIC compiler)

Available for:

The Software Exchange
P.O. Box 68
Milford, NH 03055
TRS-80 Model I Level II with
cassette; TRS-80 Model I Level II,
32K, expansion interface and disk
drive.

C Interpreter (based on the Bell Labs Language)

TINY C
(interpreter)

Available for:

Tiny-C Associates
P.O. Box 269
Holmdel, NJ 07733
Unmodified CP/M; TRS-80 MOD I
DOS.

C Compiler (based on the Bell Labs Language)

C COMPILER
(BDS)

Available for:

Lifeboat Associates
2248 Broadway
New York, NY 10024
212-580-0082
TELEX 66 8585
Unmodified CP/M; Modified TRS-80
CP/M.

COBOL (Common Business Oriented Language)

COBOL-80 (COMPILER)	Microsoft 10800 NE 8th, Suite 819 Bellevue, WA 98004 206-455-8080 TELEX 32 8945
Available for:	Unmodified CP/M; Modified TRS-80 CP/M.
NEVADA COBOL (a subset of ANSI-74) COBOL; a 16K compiler)	Business Microproducts Livermore Financial Center 1838 Catalina Court Livermore, CA 94550 415-443-4876
Available for:	TRS-80 Level II Model I, expansion interface, 48K, disk and Modified CP/M.

FORTH (COMPILER—Stack oriented language)

TINY FORTH (compiler—stack oriented language) *Available for:*	The Software Farm Box 2304 Dept A-21 Reston, VA 22090 TRS-80 Mod I cassette only.
APPLE FORTH (Compiler language stack oriented)	Programma International, Inc. 3400 Wilshire Blvd. Los Angeles, CA 90010 213-384-0579 213-384-1116 213-384-1117
Available for:	APPLE II, 16K, Cassette; APPLE II, 32K, Disk II.
MMSFORTH Interpreter and compiler)	Miller Microcomputer Services 61 Lake Shore Road Natick, MA 01760 617-663-6136
Available for:	TRS-80 Model I cassette; TRS-80 Model I DOS.

PETFORTH   Programma International, Inc.
(Compiler language   3400 Wilshire Blvd.
stack oriented)   Los Angeles, CA 90010
                           213-384-0579
                           213-384-1116
                           213-384-1117
Available for: CBM/PET, 16K Cassette.

TRS-80FORTH   Programma International Inc.
(compiler language   3400 Wilshire Blvd.
stack oriented)   Los Angeles, CA 90010
                           213-384-0579
                           213-384-1116
                           213-384-1117
Available for: TRS-80 Level Ii Model I, 16K,
                           cassette.

FORTRAN (Compiler—Formula Translation Language)

Apple FORTRAN   Apple Computer Inc.
(compiler) 3rd QTR 1980   10260 Bandley Drive
                           Cupertino, CA 95014
                           408-996-1010
Available for: APPLE II, APPLE Language
                           System, DISK II (recommended
                           system would have 2 drives).

FORTRAN-80   Microsoft
(Compiler)   10800 NE 8th, Suite 819
                           Bellevue, WA 98004
                           206-453-8080
                           TELEX 32 8945
Available for: Unmodified CP/M; Modified TRS-80
                           CP/M; TRS-80 MOD. I DOS.

LISP (Compiler—List Processing Language)

MuSIMP/muMATH-79   Microsoft
                    10800 NE 8th, Suite 819
                    Bellevue, WA 98004
                    206-455-8080
                    TELEX 32 8945

Sophisticated mathematics package useful for solving equations and simplifying formulas. Performs symbolic integration and differentiation, finite precision integer arithmetic, symbolic matrix inversion, and exact arithmetic. Useful in teaching arithmetic through calculus.
Available for: Unmodified CP/M.

muLISP   Microsoft
                             10800 NE 8th, Suite 819
                             Bellevue, WA 98004
                             206-455-8080
                             TELEX 32 8945

The language commonly used for artificial intelligence projects and in particular for list processing.
Available for: Unmodified CP/M.

TLC-LISP   The LISP CO.
                             P.O. Box 487
                             Redwood City, CA 95044
Available for: Unmodified CP/M (mem size unknown).

PASCAL *(Compiler-structured language)*

People's PASCAL I   Computer Information
("tiny" compiler—subset   Exchange, Inc.
of PASCAL)   Box 158
                             San Luis Rey, CA 92068

This language is found on tape 3 and was written by John Alexander of Berwick, Australia. Compiles slowly but has instructions on converting to disk.
Available for: TRS-80 Level II, 16K, cassette.

TRS-80 People's   Computer Information Exchange
PASCAL ("tiny"   Box 158
compiler version—   San Luis Rey, CA 92068
a subset of PASCAL)

This language version was developed by Chung and Yuen. It is oriented toward cassette sortage and is tape No. 6.
Available for: TRS-80 Level II Model I, 16K, cassette

TINY PASCAL   Supersoft Associated
(compiler)   P.O. Box 1628
                            Champaign, IL 61820
                            217-344-7596
Available for: Unmodified CP/M; TRS-80 MOD I
                            DOS.

INTEGER PASCAL   M & M Software Co.
(Compiler)   380 N. Armando, # 2-19
                            Anaheim, CA 92806

Includes compiler and interpreter; translator available
Available for: APPLE II, 48K & DISK.

Apple PASCAL   Apple Computer Inc.
(Compiler and disk   10260 Bandley Drive
operating system)   Cupertino, CA 95014
                            408-996-1010
Available for: Apple II, 48K, Disk II, (recom-
                            mended system would have 2 drives).

OMSI PASCAL VI.2   OREGON SOFTWARE
                            2340 S.W. Canyon Rd.
                            Portland, Oregon 97201
                            503-226-7760
                            TWX: 910-464-4779
Available for: Unmodified CP/M.

PASCAL/M   Digital Marketing
(compiler)   2670 Cherry Lane
                            Walnut Creek, CA 94956
                            415-938-2880
Available for: Unmodified CP/M.

PASCAL/MT   MT Microsystems/Lifeboat
                            1562 Kings Cross Drive
                            Cardiff, CA 92007
                            714-753-4856
Available for: Unmodified CP/M;Modified TRS-80
                            CP/M.

SUPERPASCAL   Ithaca Intersystems, Inc.
(PASCAL Z)   1650 Hanshaw Road

(Compiler)   P.O. Box 91
                               Ithaca, NY 14850
                               607-257-0190
                               TWX: 51 0255 4346
Available for: Unmodified CP/M.

UCSD PASCAL   Softech Microsystems
(Compiler and DOS)   9494 Black Mountain Road
                               San Diego, CA 92126
                               714-578-6105
                               TWX: 910-335-1594
Available for: Unmodified CP/M (48K).

UCSD PASCAL   FMG Corporation
(Compiler)   P.O. Box 16020
                               Fort Worth, TX 76133
                               817-294-2510
Available for: TRS-80 Level II Model I, expansion
                               interface, 48K only, disk.

UCSD PASCAL   PCD Systems
                               323 Keuka Street
                               Penn Yan, NY 14527
                               315-536-3734
Available for: TRS-80 Model II.

Disk Operating Systems

Apple II Disk Operating Systems

CP/M   Microsoft
(Modified for use on   Consumer Products
Apple Disk II)   10800 NE 8th, Suite 507
                               Bellevue, WA 98004
                               206-454-1315

This version uses a Z-80 processor accessory card for the Apple II
and included Microsoft Disk BASIC. This BASIC is easily one of
the most powerful on the market.

Available for:	Apple II, 48K, Disk II (recommended systems would have two disk drives).

DOS 3.3 (disk operating system) 3rd Qtr 1980	Apple Computer Inc. 10260 Bandley Drive Cupertino, CA 95014 408-996-1010
Available for:	Apple II, 32K, extra PROMS (included in DOS 3.3 kit), and Disk II.

OSS (disk operating system)	Optimized Systems Software Shepardson Microsystems Inc. 20395 Pacifica Dr., Suite 108A Cupertino, CA 95014 408-257-9900

Available as a disk operating system, a BASIC, a file handler, and an assembler.

Available for:	APPLE II 48K with disk.

SORCERER Disk Operating Systems

CP/M (Unmodified)	Lifeboat Associates 2248 Broadway New York, NY 10024 212-580-0082 TELEX 22 0501
Available for:	SORCERER, 32K-48K, Micropolis MOD I disk drive (¼"); SORCERER, 32K-48K, Micropolis MOD II disk drive (¼"); SORCERER, 32K-48K, Vista disk drive (¼"); SORCERER, 32K-48K, MICROMATION 8" disk drive.

MDOS	Micropolis Corporation 7959 Deering Avenue Canoga Park, CA 91304 213-703-1121

Includes an interesting version of Microsoft BASIC.

Available for:	SORCERER, 32K-48K, expansion

interface and MICROPOLIS MOD I
OR MOD II disk drives.

TRS-80 Disk Operating Systems

NEWDOS
(disk operating system
and disk modifications
for assembler/editor)
Available for:

APPARAT
7310 E. Princeton Ave.
Denver, CO 80237
303-741-1778
TRS-80 Level II Model I, expansion
interface, 32K, disk.

NEWDOS/80
(disk operating system,
assembler/editor
modifications

APPARAT
7310 E. Princeton Ave.
Denver, CO 80237
303-741-1778

Allows variable record lengths, mix or match drives (35, 40, or 77
track drives), 8″ drives, security boot up.
Available for: TRS-80 Level II Model I, expansion
interface, 32K-48K disk.

TRS-80 CP/M
(modified CP/M
disk operating system)

Available for:

Small System Software
P.O. Box 366
Newbury Park, CA 91320
LIFEBOAT Associates
2248 Broadway Suite 34
New York, NY 10024
212-580-0082
TRS-80 Level II Model I, expansion
interface, disk, 16K-48K.

CP/M
(modified CP/M
disk operating system)

Available for:

FMG Corporation
P.O. Box 16020
Fort Worth, TX 76133
817-294-2510
TRS-80 Level II Model I, expansion
interface, 16K-48K, disk.

TPM
(disk operating system-
runs CP/M programs
also)

Computer Design Labs
342 Columbus Avenue
Trenton, NJ 08629
609-599-2146

Available for:	TRS-80 Model I, 32K-48K expansion interface and disk; TRS-80 Model II.

Editor/Assembler Systems

Assembler	Quality Software
	6660 Reseda Blvd. Suite 105
	Reseda, CA 91335
	213-344-6599
Available for:	Atari 400/800, cassette.
CO-RESIDENT ASSEMBLER	Microproducts
	1024 17th Street
	Hermosa Beach, CA 90254
Available for:	APPLE II, 16K, cassette.
EDITOR/ASSEMBLER PLUS	Microsoft
Available for:	TRS-80 Level II Model I 16K.
LISA INTERACTIVE ASSEMBLER	Programma International, Inc.
	3400 Wilshire Blvd.
	Los Angeles, CA 90010
	213-384-0579
	213-384-1116
	213-384-1117
Available for:	APPLE II, 32K, Disk II.
MACRO-80 (ASSEMBLER)	Microsoft
	Consumer Products
	10800 NE 8th, Suite 507
	Bellevue, WA 98004
	206-454-1315
Available for:	Unmodified CP/M; Modified TRS-80 CP/M; TRS-80 MOD I DOS.
EDIT-80 (EDITOR)	Microsoft
	Consumer Products
	10800 NE 8th, Suite 507
	Bellevue, WA 98004
	206-454-1315
Available for:	Unmodified CP/M; Modified TRS-80 CP/M; TRS-80 MOD I DOS.

MACRO ASSEMBLER/ EDITOR	Eastern House Software
	3239 Linda Drive
	Winston-Salem, NC 27106
Available for:	CBM/PET, Cassette; CBM/PET, 32K and 2040 Disk system; APPLE II, Cassette; APPLE II, Disk II; ATARI, Cassette.

S-C ASSEMBLER II	S-C Software
	P.O.Box 5537
	Richardson, TX 75080
Available for:	Apple II, 16K, Cassette.

6 CHARACTER Label Assembler/Editor	Microproducts
	2107 Artesia Blvd.
	Redondo Beach, CA 90278
	213-374-1673
Available for:	Apple II, 32K - 48K and Disk II.

Utilities

APPLE-DOC (a documenting editor)	Southwestern Data Systems
	P.O.Box 582-M
	Santree, CA 92071
	714-562-3670

Allows global editing of Applesoft Basic programs and the generation of a variables cross listing.

Available for:	APPLE II, APPLESOFT and Cassette; APPLE II, APPLESOFT and Disk.

CMDSTR* (creates and executes a disk file of commands through one command or AUTO. Boot into BASIC and program.)	ELCOMPCO
	P.O. Box 6133
	Albany, CA 94706

DOSDMD*   *All on the same cassette
(Submit a list of DOS commands at one time)

COPYFILE*
(Allows single disk user to copy file from one disk to another—
TRSDOS 2.2, TRSDOS 2.3)

Available for: TRS-80 Model I Level II, 16-48K,
                  expansion interface and disk drive.

DAKINS UTILITIES   Dakins Corporation
(Useful programs for   P.O.Box 21187
disk/file copy, disk   Denver, CO 80221
patching etc.—technical) 303-426-6090
Available for: APPLE II, 48K, 2 Disk II's and
                       Printer.

DIAGNOSTICS I   Supersoft Associates
(Operational tests   P.O.Box 1628
for computer system)   Champaign, IL 61820
                       217-344-7596
                       217-384-0847 (Technical Hot Line)
Available for: Unmodified CP/M; TRS-80 MOD I
                       DOS.

FILETRAN   Business Microproducts
(converts TRSDOS files Livermore Financial Center
to CP/M files, converts 1838 Catalina Court
Level II BASIC state- Livermore, CA 94550
ments to Microsoft   415-449-4412
MBASIC TRSDOS and
CP/M directories)
Available for: TRS-80 Model I Level II, 32K,
                       expansion interface, disk drive, and
                       CP/M disk operating system as well
                       as TRSDOS.

FINDISK II   Documan Software
(master catalog program Box 38-A
to show contents of all Kalamazoo, MI 49005
your disks)   616-344-0805
Available for: TRS-80 Model I Level II 32K, expan-
                       sion interface and disk drive.

MASTER CATALOG   Elliam Associates
FOR CP/M   2400 Bessemer Street

(keeps track of all   Woodland Hills, CA 91367
files on all diskettes)
Available for: Unmodified CP/M.

PROGRAMMER'S   Southwestern Data Systems
UTILITY PACK   P.O.Box 582-M
(Miscellaneous useful but   Santree, CA 92071
somewhat technical   714-562-3670
programs)
Available for: APPLE II Cassette; APPLE II Disk.

RX (disk version)   The Software Exchange
                             6 South Street, Box 68
                             Milford, NH 03055
                             603-673-5144
Available for: TRS-80 Level II Model I, 32K,
                             expansion interface and 1 disk.

SINGLE DRIVE COPY   Progressive Software
(Diskette Copy Program)   P.O.Box 273
                             Plymouth Meeting, PA 19462
Available for: APPLE II, 32K, Disk II, DOS 3.2.

UTILITY PACK   Progressive Software
(useful programs for disk   P.O.Box 273
file maintenance)   Plymouth Meeting, PA 19462

Allows automatic conversion of Integer Basic program to Apple-
soft format, appending 2 Integer Basic into single program,
Integer Basic program copier, and binary program copy routine.
Available for: APPLE II and Disk II.

CHAPTER 14

Resources: Books, Available Program Guides and Sources of Educational Programs

Many books are available on computers, languages, lists, available programs, and technical information on the processor "chips" and accessory "chips" (circuits) used in microcomputers.

The resources listed in this chapter are a selected representation of the available field. The only technical books listed are those which could be useful in specialized programing on your microcomputer. No books on the hardware of microcomputers are listed. This list is divided as follows:

1. General Books—ranges from general speculative literature through easy-to-use programing books on BASIC to books on profiting from use of your microcomputer. The book on profit-making is presented for its programing techniques rather than the profit potential.

2. Computer Language Books—ranges from a book on using the CP/M disk operating system (a must) through books on programing in BASIC, COBOL, PASCAL, and FORTRAN to a book that compares and shows the features of the various dialects of BASIC. This last book is very useful if you need to know how to convert a program written in one BASIC dialect to another.

3. Books of Programs—ranges from games through simulations to useful general purpose programs.

4. Available Program Guides—bibliographies and source lists of programs for microcomputers.

5. Technical but Useful Books—ranges from books on how to create graphics, through using special software capabilities built into the microcomputer, to a book showing how to retrieve program and data thought to be forever lost on a disk.

6. Computer Education and Literacy Materials—ranges from computer lessons on cassette through a computer literacy course with filmstrips to a set of eight videocassettes on microcomputers.

7. Selected Sources of Educational Software—presents the companies known to the author which have concentrated on educational software or companies which have a fair number of good educational programs for microcomputers.

8. School/Media Applications

Each month brings new announcements of books, equipment, languages, and companies offering microcomputer programs; tis resource list can at best be a starting point.

General Books

Basic and the Personal Computer, Thomas A. Dwyer and Margot Critchfield. Addison-Wesley: Reading, Mass., 1978, 438 pp.

The Best of Creative Computing Vol. 1. David H. Ahl (Ed.). Creative Computing Press: Morristown, N.J., 1976, 316 pp.

The Best of Creative Computing Vol. 2, David H. Ahl (Ed.). Creative Computing Press: Morristown, N.J., 1977, 323 pp.

The Best of Micro Vol. 1 (Kim, Pet, Apple). Micro: Chelmsford, Mass.

The Best of Micro Vol. 2 (Kim, Pet, Apple). Micro: Chelmsford, Mass.

Computer Applications in Instruction: A Teacher's Guide to Selection and Use. Judith B. Edwards, Antoinette S. Ellis, Duane E. Richardson, Donald Holznagel, and Daniel Klassen. Time Share (a Houghton Mifflin Company): Hanover, N.H., 1978, 202 pp.

Computer Lib Dream Machines, Theodor H. Nelson. Hugo's Book Service: Chicago, Ill., 1974, 127 pp.

How to Profit from Your Personal Computer, T.C. Lewis. Hayden Book Co., Inc.: Rochelle Park, N.J. 1978, 191 pp.

Microcomputers and the 3R's: A Guide for Teachers, Christine Doeer. Hayden Book Company, Inc.: Rochelle Park, N.J., 1979, 177 pp.

The Mind Appliance: Home Computer Applications, T.G. Lewis. Hayden Book Co., Inc.: Rochelle Park, N.J., 1978, 137 pp.

Peanut Butter and Jelly Guide to Computers, Jerry Willis, Dilithium Press, Forrest Grove, Oreg., 1978, 225 pp. ISBN 0-918398-13-4.

Robots on Your Doorstep, Nels Winkless and Iben Browning. Robotics Press: Portland, Oreg., 1978, 179 pp.

Running Wild—The Next Industrial Revolution, Adam Osborne. Osborne/McGraw-Hill, Inc.: Berkeley, Calif., 1979, 181 pp.

Computer Language Books

The Basic Handbook, David A. Lien. Compu-Soft Publishing: San Diego, 1979, 360 pp. Covers more than 50 dialects of BASIC. ISBN 0-932760-00-7.

Beginner's Manual for the UCSD PASCAL System, Kenneth L. Bowles. McGraw-Hill, Inc.: Berkeley, 1980. ISBN 0-07-006745-7.

The BYTE Book of PASCAL, Blaise W. Liffick (ed.). Byte Books Division,

McGraw-Hill, Inc.: Berkeley, Calif., 1980.

How to Get Started with CP/M, Carl Townsend. Dilithium Press: Forrest Grove, Oreg., 1979. ISBN 0-918398-32-0.

My Computer Likes Me When I Speak BASiC, Bob Albrecht. Dilithium Press: Forrest Grove, Oreg., 1972, 61 pp. ISBN 0-198138-12-6.

PASCAL USER Manual and Report (2nd Edition). Jensen and Wirth. Springer-Verlag: New York, N.Y., 1975. ISBN 0-387-90144-2.

Programming in PASCAL, Peter Grogono. Addison Wesley: Reading, Mass., 1978. ISBN 0-201-02473-X.

A Simplified Guide to Fortran Programing, Daniel McCracken. John Wiley & Sons: New York, N.Y., 1974. ISBN O-471-58293-X.

Structured COBOL, Ruth Ashley. John Wiley & Sons, Inc.: New York, N.Y., Apr. 1980, 320 pp. ISBN 0-471-05362-7.

TRS-80 BASIC, Bob Albrecht and Don Inman. John Wiley & Sons, Inc: New York, N.Y.

Books of Programs

102 Basic Games, David H. Ahl (Ed.). Creative Computing Press: Morristown, N.J., 1978.

More Basic Computer Games, Creative Computing Press: Morristown, N.J., 192 pp.

Some Common BASIC Programs, Adam Osborne Associates, Inc.: Berkeley, Calif., 1978, 192 pp. (The programs in the book are also available on cassette for the PET and the TRS-80.)

80 Programs for the TRS-80, Jim Perry and Chris Brown (ed.). 1001001, Inc.: Peterborough, N.H., 1979, Second printing, 234 pp. (These programs are in TRS-80 BASIC and generally could be adapted to other BASICs.)

Available Program Guides

Apple II Software Directory: Vol 2. Games, Demo, and Utility, WIDL Video: Chicago, Ill. 1979, 45 pp.

Technical But Useful Books

Inside Level II: A Guide to the Effective Use of Your TRS-80 ROM, John Blattner. Mumford Micro Systems, Box 435-E, Summerland, CA 93067. 805-969-4557.

Introduction to TRS-80 Graphics, Bob Albrecht and Don Inman. Dilithium Press: Forrest Grove, Oreg., 1979. ISBN 0-918398-18-5.
TRS-80 Disassembled Handbook, R.M. Richardson. Richfield Engineering Ltd: Chautauqua, N.Y., 1980, 60 pp.
TRS-80 Disk and Other Mysteries, H.C.Pennington. International Jewelry Guild, Inc.: Upland, Calif., 1979. ISBN 0-936200-00-6.

Computer Education and Literacy Materials

Computer Programing: BASIC for Microcomputers

Educational Activities, Inc.
P.O.Box 392
Freeport, NY 11520

A step-by-step computer literacy course. Includes color sound filmstrips and comprehensive teachers guide.

Little Computers . . . See How They Run
A series of 8 videocassette education programs.

EVOLUTION 1
Electronic Data Systems
Corp. Center
7171 Forest Lane
Dallas, TX 75230
800-527-0278

Plus Teaching Pac
Seventeen lessons used
to teach the most frequently
used BASIC statements.

Charles Mann & Associates
Micro Software Division
Customer Relations Branch
7594 San Remo Trail
Yucca Valley, CA 92284
714-365-9718

Available for: APPLE II, 32K, Disk II.

The Teacher Plus
Lessons are used to teach
the basics while complex
examples are available in
running form. (17 lessons)

Charles Mann & Associates
Micro Software Division
Customer Relations Branch
7594 San Remo Trail
Yucca Valley, CA 92284
714-365-9718

Available for: APPLE II, 32K, Disk II.

Sources of Educational Software

The alta Experience
(educational courseware)

Micro Power & Light Co.
1108 Keystone, Dept. C
13773 N. Central Expressway
Dallas, TX 75243
214-234-8233

Covers mathematics, spelling,
grammar, map reading, scientific method, critical reasoning,
the human body, memory
enhancement.
Available for: APPLE II.

Apple II Library
(a large number of educational
programs designed for the
Apple II with Disk II)

MECC Instructional Services
Division
2520 Broadway Drive
Lauderdale, MN 55113

A wide-ranging set of instruc-
tional programs developed
through the statewide Minnesota
Educational Computing
Consortium.
See the 1979-80 Microcomputer
Report of the Minnesota Educa-
tional Computing Consortium.

*BASIC programs for
Education*
Covers biology, chemistry economics, education, geography
humanities, management scien-
ces, mathematics, physics, politi-
cal science, statistics, psychology
and sociology.
Available for: APPLE II and Disk II; CBM/PET 8K; TRS-80
Model I, Level II, 32K expansion interface and disk.
See also: *Pipeline* (the CONDUIT newsletter)

CONDUIT
Iowa City, IA

EUCLID

A theorem-proving program
which allows high school
geometry students to work at
their own rate. EUCLID represents artificially intelligent
computer-assisted instruction
written in extended BASIC.
Program Listing Cost: about
$2.00 payable to Taylor Allerdice
High School
Description: Theorem proving
with EUCLID, Kelanic, Thomas
J. *Creative Computing*,
July 1978, 60-63.

Thomas J. Kelanic
Taylor Allderdice High School
2409 Shady Avenue
Pittsburgh, PA 15217

Children's education for TRS-80
Level II 16K—PLAYFUL
PROFESSOR—tutoring in
integer mathematics and fractions in graphic game style.

Med Systems
P.O.Box 2675
Chapel Hill, NC 27415

MONEY MASTER
covers counting of paper money
and coins in a graphic game
format.

*Educational Software for
TRS-80* (80+ programs)
elementary, biology, science,
accounting, math, history,
economics, foreign language,
business ed., geography, games

Micro Learningware
Box 2134
North Mankato, MN 56001
507-625-2205

*Educational Software for
TRS-80 LII-4K*

Mercer Systems, Inc.
87 Scooter Lane
Hicksville, NY 11801

ALPHA—ages 4-7—
to teach alphabet recognition
(cassette)

SIGMA—grades 1-3 produces
random series of single digit
addition problems (of form $3 + 5 = 8$)
(cassette)

PET Professor   Cow Bay Computing
(70-lesson package on math   Box 515
operations—whole numbers,   Manhasset, NY 11030
fraction, and decimals)
Available for: CBM/PET, 16K, cassette; CBM/PET, 32K, Disk

Education Software   Cook's ComputerCo.
                                         1905 Bailey Dr.
                                         Marshalltown, IA 50158

School Media Applications

The Microcomputer and the School Media Specialist, Pierre P. Barrette.
    Libraries Unlimited, Inc.: Littleton, Col., 1980 (summer), 200 pp.